THE
PERFECT
ASSESSMENT
— SYSTEM —

THE
PERFECT
ASSESSMENT
— SYSTEM —

RICK STIGGINS

Alexandria, Virginia USA

1703 N. Beauregard St. • Alexandria, VA 22311-1714 USA
Phone: 800-933-2723 or 703-578-9600 • Fax: 703-575-5400
Website: www.ascd.org • E-mail: member@ascd.org
Author guidelines: www.ascd.org/write

Deborah S. Delisle, *Executive Director;* Robert D. Clouse, *Managing Director, Digital Content & Publications;* Stefani Roth, *Publisher;* Genny Ostertag, *Director, Content Acquisitions;* Julie Houtz, *Director, Book Editing & Production;* Katie Martin, *Editor;* Khanh Pham, *Graphic Designer;* Mike Kalyan, *Director, Production Services;* Valerie Younkin, *Production Designer;* Andrea Hoffman, *Senior Production Specialist*

PAPERBACK ISBN: 978-1-4166-2381-6   ASCD product #117079   n3/17

PDF E-BOOK ISBN: 978-1-4166-2383-0; see Books in Print for other formats.

Quantity discounts are available: e-mail programteam@ascd.org or call 800-933-2723, ext. 5773, or 703-575-5773. For desk copies, go to www.ascd.org/deskcopy.

Library of Congress Cataloging-in-Publication Data
Names: Stiggins, Richard J., author.
Title: The perfect assessment system / Rick Stiggins.
Description: Alexandria, VA : ASCD, [2017] | Includes bibliographical references and index.
Identifiers: LCCN 2016057226 (print) | LCCN 2017008286 (ebook) | ISBN 9781416623816 (pbk.) | ISBN 9781416623830 (PDF)
Subjects: LCSH: Educational tests and measurements--United States. | Motivation in education--United States.
Classification: LCC LB3051 .S8538 2017 (print) | LCC LB3051 (ebook) | DDC 371.26--dc23
LC record available at https://lccn.loc.gov/2016057226

26 25 24 23 22 21 20 19 18 17   1 2 3 4 5 6 7 8 9 10 11 12

In memory of my beloved Nancy

THE PERFECT ASSESSMENT SYSTEM

FOREWORD

by W. James Popham

History tells us that the status quo simply loves to be preserved. Our inclination to avoid messing with the status quo is confirmed when we hear such adages as "If it ain't broke, don't fix it!" or "The old ways are the good ways." Most people, it appears, prefer things to stay pretty much the way they currently are.

The attitude most authors take toward educational testing in the United States bears this out. It's apparent in the suggestions that mildly miffed critics of our assessment system offer for attainable yet modest improvements. "Tinker with the status quo ever so lightly," they say, "but don't seriously depart from it."

But a genuinely vexed author, one who is fundamentally fed up with the status quo, is sometimes driven to advocate jettisoning an entire enterprise and boldly starting afresh. That's what Rick Stiggins does, and with gusto, in this exciting denunciation of what he regards as our obsolete school testing system. Based on a four-decade career soaking in educational assessment's status quo, he has now concluded its shortcomings are so severe that what we need is nothing short of a complete reinvention of testing culture and practices.

As Stiggins makes clear early on, the many misuses of educational tests are now suffocating us to such a degree that it's time to start over. After laying out a litany of deficits in the way we currently use tests in our districts, schools, and classrooms, he identifies a set of "troubling realities" that have triggered those problems. But then—and this represents his book's chief contribution—Stiggins provides the framework for a do-over: an approach to testing that he modestly labels *the perfect assessment system*. The remainder of the book is devoted to a crisp spell-out of what this perfection looks like and what it would take for us to achieve it.

I know Rick Stiggins well and have for a long time. We first met about 40 years ago and, as fate would dictate, we now live about 15 minutes from each other just south of Portland, Oregon. Given that proximity, we meet about once a month over breakfast to exchange views on the current crises in the educational testing world. (For the record, I end up paying for breakfast more than 75 percent of the time—a statistically significant difference.) And so I know with certainty that when he describes his recommended approach to school testing as the perfect assessment system, he recognizes the challenge of installing even an *improved* testing system, much less a *perfect* one.

What he presents to us in this thought-provoking book is a *vision* of perfection—one that supplies tangible targets for those who wish to bring about a transformation of today's educational testing, and one with a simplicity that belies its potential to enhance student well-being.

The foundation for his perfect assessment system is Stiggins's conviction that the purpose of assessment must always be clear. *What will this test be measuring? Will the results be used to support student learning, or will the results be used to certify whether or not learning has occurred? Who will use the results, and what decisions will they make based on these results?* If these questions seem like obvious ones, remember that, in this nation, we have leaned heavily on large-scale standardized tests for almost a full century, yet enormous confusion persists regarding whether educational tests are really intended to support learning or to evaluate instructional quality. For Stiggins, designation of purpose—and a corollary isolation of the decisions to be influenced by test results—is mandatory.

His vision includes several other ingredients beyond purpose determination. One of these is the requirement that all educational tests satisfy standards of assessment quality so that the evidence these tests elicit will be defensibly accurate. Stiggins spells out clearly what's needed for a test to elicit accurate evidence of students' achievement—whether that test is administered at the state, district, or classroom level. Moreover, he wants educators and policymakers to be sufficiently assessment literate so that they can not only gauge the quality of the educational tests being used but also accurately interpret the results those tests yield.

Further, Stiggins's conception of a perfect assessment enterprise incorporates time-tested principles of effective communication. He advocates that teachers and school administrators acquire sufficient levels of assessment literacy so that they can communicate students' test results in a truly comprehensible manner to parents, to the public, and to all others who rely on such test-based evidence.

And finally, invoking a theme that has governed his thinking for most of his career, Stiggins wants us to make sure that our assessment practices are linked to students' motivation in a manner that engenders student self-esteem rather than damages it. More than any other writer, Stiggins has reminded us over the years that if our educational tests lead too many students to conclude that they're not smart or capable enough and that school success is hopelessly out of their reach, then the entire use of educational testing is dysfunctional. This book's focus on using classroom tests *for* students' learning rather than as tests *of* students' learning is a helpful reminder.

Rick Stiggins was trained as a traditional educational measurement specialist at Michigan State University, one of the United States' strongest centers of graduate psychometric training. Yet, after a decade or so of traditional measurement work, his attention shifted from large-scale testing to studying the instructional dividends of classroom assessment. Indeed, for several decades, while the educational measurement community was caught up with the high-stakes applications of large-scale standardized testing, Stiggins almost single-handedly championed the instructional dividends of appropriate teacher-made classroom testing. Here he maintains, rightfully, that the most powerful assessment-informed decisions are those made in the classroom and calls for a system designed, above all, to support the work of teachers and their students.

The lessons learned from an entire career in educational testing have been coalesced effectively in *The Perfect Assessment System*'s call for an across-the-board assessment revolution. It is time, Stiggins asserts, to discard testing's traditional "best practices" and start again—from scratch.

Only frustrated and angry writers are willing to dump the status quo so totally in a quest for something better. Thank heavens Rick Stiggins is sufficiently frustrated and angry.

W. James Popham
Professor Emeritus
UCLA Graduate School of Education and Information Studies
October 2016

CONFRONTING OUR ASSESSMENT CRISIS: IT'S TIME TO START OVER

If measurement is to continue to play an increasingly important role in education, those who measure must be more than technicians. Unless their efforts are directed by a sound educational philosophy, unless they accept and welcome a greater share of responsibility for the selection and clarification of educational objectives, unless they show much more concern with what they measure as well as with how they measure it, much of their work will prove futile and ineffective.

—E. F. LINDQUIST

In this book, I call for the ground-up redevelopment of assessment in American education. I describe why this is necessary and how to go about it in specific detail. But I want readers to understand from the outset both the experiences and resulting value perspectives (perhaps even moral code) that give rise to the vision I present.

First, I was a struggling learner in my public schooling years. My experiences taught me how devastating hopelessness can be in the classroom and why it's so important for every learner to believe in the possibility of his or her success.

Second, I have spent my career in educational measurement studying and working in classrooms with students and teachers, watching very expensive standardized testing processes unfold in ways that rarely supported the

1

learning that was going on in those classrooms. Policymakers have paid little attention and allocated virtually no resources in support of the classroom level of assessment, where its power to enhance learning is unlimited.

Third, I have worked extensively with local school leaders as they have tried to succeed in politicized assessment environments within which they have little understanding and over which they have no control. They long for assessment pathways to improved teaching, learning, and student well-being, and they find few.

In this book, I speak for all learners who hope to succeed, for the teachers who want them to succeed, and for local school leaders whose aspirations for success have been thwarted by our assessment traditions.

WHERE WE STAND

Systems of educational testing in U.S. schools are in crisis. Our newest federal school improvement legislation, the Every Student Succeeds Act (ESSA), acknowledges as much by inviting state and local educational agencies to explore alternate, innovative uses of assessment. This amounts to a confession that federally mandated assessment practices intended to improve schools are not doing the job. They are compromising student learning and damaging the social institution we call "school." An assessment crisis that has been simmering for decades is finally boiling over, and the time has come to take overdue and assertive action to improve both specific testing practices and our entire assessment culture.

Just to be clear, the focus of my concern goes far deeper than our national and statewide standardized testing practices, although these certainly are in desperate need of deep rethinking and improvement. However, even more troubling problems plague our local district, school, and classroom assessment systems and practices. Consider the big picture:

- There is a national "opt out" movement led by parents to withdraw their children from high-stakes testing programs because they see no educational value in these tests. These parents fear (and some report) that the emphasis on high-stakes testing is emotionally damaging to their children.

- Parents have filed lawsuits in response to local school administrators' efforts to punish students who opt out of end-of-year testing by requiring that they repeat the grade regardless of their level of achievement.
- Students who see little instructional relevance in the high-stakes tests they are required to take are protesting with signs that read "Hands up, don't test" and are refusing to take the tests.
- Issues related to matters of equity are being raised by minority parents and their allies. Some favor annual test-score reporting in order to maintain a spotlight on unequal opportunities for minority children, while others worry about test bias and tests that are insensitive to non-majority cultures.
- Professional educators are losing their jobs and even being sentenced to years in prison for cheating on standardized tests. They claim that their supervisors made them do it.
- States continue to withdraw from multistate assessment consortiums of standardized test development. They are searching for better alternatives.
- Educational policy leaders, such as Achieve and the Council of Chief State School Officers, offer states guidelines for conducting audits of local assessment systems that focus almost exclusively on standardized accountability testing and provide little advice for monitoring the quality of classroom-level assessment, even though the classroom is where the vast majority of assessment takes place.
- Newly minted national standards of test quality developed jointly and promulgated by the American Educational Research Association, the American Psychological Association, and the National Council on Measurement in Education (2014) address matters of sound standardized testing and bypass specifics of sound classroom assessment.

These circumstances may have risen, at least in part, from the following troubling realities:

- While ESSA offers assessment flexibility, that flex is in state accountability testing programs, perpetuating the poorly informed, decades-long federal belief that the best way to use testing to improve schools is to hold schools accountable for raising annual test scores.

- As a result of this kind of federal leadership, an entire generation of school leaders and policymakers have come to see assessment primarily as an accountability tool instead of a powerful means of supporting student learning.

- Most teachers—novices and veterans alike—have not been given the opportunity to understand or to learn to apply basic principles of sound classroom assessment.

- Preparation programs for school administrators remain devoid of relevant, helpful assessment training, leaving teachers with no one to turn to for help if they need or want it.

- Consequently, even though ESSA offers states and local school districts the opportunity to remake their assessment systems in new and productive ways, those who would lead the development and implementation of such potentially exciting systems often lack the assessment literacy needed to do so effectively.

- Naïve federal, state, and local policymakers reveal a profound lack of assessment literacy by setting policies requiring that changes in annual standardized test scores be used to evaluate the performance of teachers and their supervisors despite the fact that this amounts to an indefensible application of those scores for a wide variety of technical and practical reasons (Stiggins, 2014b).

- Since 2010, the United States has spent hundreds of millions of dollars developing new multistate standardized tests whose scores are of little direct instructional value. Local teachers, school leaders, and even assessment personnel are struggling to figure out what to do with all these very expensive results (Oregon Department of Education, 2016).

- Test publishers have been bypassing professional educators altogether and selling their products directly to untrained legislators, turning testing into an increasingly political and financial enterprise versus a tool for teaching and learning.

How can something so critical to the success of our schooling process be going so terribly wrong? The simplest answer is that there is a profound lack of understanding of the basic principles of sound assessment practice throughout the fabric of American educational policy and practice. *Assessment is the process of gathering evidence of student learning to inform educational decisions.* Student success hinges on the quality of those decisions, and the quality of those decisions depends on the quality of the evidence (assessment results) upon which they are based. U.S. students are at risk because our national, state, local district, school, and classroom assessment systems very often do *not* yield the kinds of evidence required for sound instructional decision making where it really matters: in the classroom. Typically, these systems provide only gross indicators of student achievement that cannot inform the classroom-level instructional decisions that truly drive school quality. This has been the case for decades. And yet, over the decades, practitioners and school communities have witnessed layer upon layer of new testing, from local to state to national to international levels. It has come at immense cost, and we have little by way of enhanced student learning to show for it. As a result, the culture surrounding assessment both within and around schools has become increasingly and profoundly toxic and destructive.

WHAT WE MUST DO

Based on my 44 years of experience in the measurement field, and in the face of this intensifying upheaval, I have become convinced that our current systems of educational assessment are so flawed at so many levels that they cannot be saved. Unless we act assertively right now to establish the instructional utility and relevance of assessment, we will continue to waste enormous amounts of resources, and the harm done to students and teachers will reach truly perilous levels.

Yet even in the face of this turmoil, we need not and indeed cannot be discouraged. I believe we have not yet begun to explore assessment's true potential to enhance school quality and student well-being. The future of assessment as a teaching and learning tool can be very bright under the right conditions. This book details those conditions. They are not currently in place in our schools and have not been for a very long time. But they can be. In the presentation that follows, I will chart a course to a new vision of excellence in assessment that promises much higher levels of student learning success at a fraction of our current testing costs.

Be advised, however, that this success will hinge on our willingness to rethink our practices and make critically important investments at two levels of our assessment infrastructure:

1. We will need to rethink why we assess, what we assess, how we assess it, and what we do with the results. We must fundamentally reconsider the specific strategies and tactics that define assessment in our schools.

2. We will need to address the assessment culture—the social and educational environment—within which we will carry out these reconsidered assessment strategies and tactics. In other words, we must assess well within the context of our societal and educational aspirations, values, and beliefs so as to promote a universal opportunity for learner success, regardless of the learner's social or economic background.

Just imagine what might happen if we broke the old molds of large-scale accountability testing, college admissions testing, and even classroom testing for grading purposes and redeveloped them from the ground up to be the very best they can be at promoting student learning. What might we create for the sake of school quality and student success if we built an entirely new assessment culture for American schools? What positive and productive systems would we create to satisfy the information needs of *all* instructional decision makers? What if we reversed our priorities and used assessment to support teaching and learning first and foremost while still managing to satisfy our accountability needs? What if these systems didn't just identify educational problems but also helped solve them? Bottom line: If we were unconstrained by our historic testing legacy, what kind of system might we create, and how would it fit within our schooling processes?

WHAT WILL A TRULY PRODUCTIVE ASSESSMENT SYSTEM LOOK LIKE?

The assessment system I advocate is relatively easy to describe. But its apparent simplicity should not lead us to underestimate its power to enhance not only *student learning* but also *student well-being*. As you will see, putting in place the conditions necessary to use assessment in *all* of its potentially powerful ways will require considerable investment in our teachers, school leaders, policymakers, and parent communities.

To begin with, a truly productive system will arise from a new culture in which there will never be confusion about our assessment purposes. In every context, we will know why we are assessing student achievement: either to (a) support student learning or (b) judge and report the sufficiency of that learning. Assessors at all levels and in all contexts will declare the instructional decision makers they intend to inform before they begin the assessment process. They will proceed with their assessment only when they know with certainty who will use the results to inform what decisions and, therefore, what information their assessment must be designed and built to provide. Our assessment systems across all levels of use, from the classroom to the boardroom, *will serve all instructional decision makers*, not just once a year but throughout instruction—*before, during, and after the learning*. To repeat for emphasis, regardless of the context, the specific purpose of each assessment will always be clear for and endorsed by all involved.

In the assessment future I am envisioning, we will make absolutely certain that *all of our valued learning targets are clear and appropriate* for the intended learners. This is as essential a foundation for sound assessment as it is for good teaching and learning! The traditional practice of creating tests that thinly sample broad domains of achievement standards will be replaced by assessments that tell us how each student is doing in mastering each priority achievement standard. This will be a completely standards-referenced assessment system informing us on all occasions and in all contexts what comes next in every student's learning. We will agree once and for all on the learning targets that we hold as important for our children and on how to assess these in instructionally relevant ways. Some achievement standards will be endorsed as important across an entire state, others by local districts, and still others by individual teachers. And, regardless of their complexity, all standards will be assessed accurately by selecting from the full range of available assessment methods.

In other words, *all assessments—whether classroom assessments, interim benchmark tests, or annual tests—will meet standards of quality* so as to yield dependable evidence to inform sound and productive instructional decision making. As a result, teachers, school leaders, parents, and students themselves will have confidence in both the utility and the benefit of assessment in all contexts.

We will lay the foundation of this system by making sure everyone involved, educator and policymaker alike, is *sufficiently assessment literate* to understand what it means to use assessment to protect and promote the well-being of students. Those who assess will know what assessment method to use when, and how to use it to yield dependable results and to help all students believe success is within reach if they keep striving. Schools and the communities they belong to will collaborate to discover and minimize the sources of bias and cultural insensitivity that can distort assessment results.

We will build our new system around *principles of effective communication of assessment results*, ensuring that those who receive the results will understand them completely and be able to use them as the catalyst for productive action. We will end a long history of sending periodic test scores or report card grades to people who have no idea what they mean, how to interpret them, or how to act on them appropriately. Practitioners will be sufficiently assessment literate to understand that feedback to students intended to promote learning differs from feedback that merely reports the sufficiency of that learning with a grade or score. We will make sure assessors convey only truly useful information that fits the instructional context.

And finally, we will *link our assessment practices to student motivation* in constructive ways that keep *all* students believing success is within reach if they keep striving for it. This means we will re-evaluate traditional reward- and punishment-driven "motivational practices" that have the effect of discouraging major segments of our student population. Fear and intimidation will give way to confidence and hope as the new emotional dynamics underpinning student motivation and learning success. The result will be an open learning environment full of equal learning opportunities for all learners, regardless of background. This represents the most profound shift in our assessment culture. In the future, we will embrace principles of assertive "assessment FOR learning" alongside assessment of learning.

In short, we will never again have to worry about testing the right "common core" things or if there's "too much standardized testing" going on. We won't be wondering if educators are cheating to inflate test scores or if some students are being cheated out of their opportunity for success. Policymakers will not be grasping clumsily at the wrong testing straws and setting truly damaging policies due to their lack of assessment literacy. In our new assessment culture, we will start over, and universal assessment competence and confidence will rule—just the opposite of circumstances today—because we will invest in it.

We know how to make all of this happen, because enlightened colleagues from countries whose assessment traditions are different from ours, as well as many outstanding teachers across the United States, have helped us summon and focus this vision of relevant, helpful assessment from the fog of assessment chaos and bewilderment. It is a vision that holds immense promise for our students. But to get there we must scrap current assessment practices and replace them with a new assessment culture of innovative priorities, policies, and practices. I call it the *"perfect* assessment system," and I've chosen this specific label for two reasons. First, I wanted to hold myself to the very highest standards as I thought through and assembled this system. Second, I believe that what follows is the only assessment plan that can satisfy all of the ideals framed in the above paragraphs.

WHY MAKE SWEEPING CHANGES NOW?

For decades we have been guilty of severely restrictive assessment "tunnel vision," thus failing to recognize, let alone tap, potent new ideas. We have also left *the student as assessment user* almost entirely out of our assessment equation. These are shameful realities we cannot ignore any longer, and there are many reasons why.

Reason 1: Schools Have a New Mission, Which Demands a New Assessment Vision.

Historically, a primary social mission of our schools has been to begin the process of sorting citizens into the various segments of our social and economic system by ranking them based on achievement by the end of high school. Assessment's traditional role has been to provide the evidence needed to grade and sort. However, due to the rapid evolution of our society in recent decades, that mission has expanded to include holding schools accountable for helping "every student succeed" at mastering the essential, lifelong learner proficiencies needed to thrive in society. Schools have been charged with making sure that *all* students, not just those at the top of the rank order, are ready for college and workplace training. Educators are being ordered to narrow achievement gaps among various subpopulations of our student body and reduce dropout rates. To achieve these goals, we must transform assessment from a one-dimensional source of evidence for sorting into a multi-dimensional tool for teaching and learning capable of motivating *all* students to aspire to and become capable lifelong learners.

Reason 2: We Have Failed to Clearly or Completely Define "Academic Success."

Our assessment traditions have not defined the meaning of academic success clearly, completely, or in practical terms, and this has had profound instructional implications.

First, those traditions have defined learning outcomes in terms of broad achievement domains. A domain is a large collection of learning targets to which we assign labels such as "reading," "math," "science," "language arts," and so on. Typically, domain labels include a grade-level reference, such as "3rd grade reading" or "5th grade math." Each domain includes targets that might be covered in a year of instruction or more.

To measure student achievement over that span, assessors write test items that provide a representative sample of the learning targets within domains. The test scores generated are intended to serve as evidence of learning and support *general* inferences regarding student mastery of the domain sampled. I emphasize general because this is a critical point. Test scores do not and currently cannot support conclusions about student mastery of any of the individual learning targets within the domain.

A variation on this theme has emerged in recent years, with learning targets taking the form of lists of achievement standards, and assessors writing test exercises to sample this array of standards. Again, the resulting total test score is said to reflect the extent of student mastery of the domain, but again, that test score does not reveal which standards were included on the test and cannot support sound conclusions as to which of the individual standards students have mastered, either individually or collectively.

The *instructional* implications of this kind of domain-sampling test design for accountability testing are clear. Scores may support inferences about levels of achievement across the domain, but they do not provide the level of detail teachers and students need to act on the results to improve learning. They need to know which targets or standards have been mastered in order to decide what comes next in the learning. As we look to our assessment future, we must build systems that guarantee that detail. The perfect system I envision will do so.

Reason 3: We Have Never Really Cared About the Quality of Our Assessments.

A high-quality assessment provides an accurate, dependable representation of student learning and does so in a form that fits the information needs of the intended users. We know how to create good assessments and use them well. The problem is that this wisdom has rarely found its way into our schools and classrooms. We haven't bothered to provide training in these matters for policymakers, for local school leaders, or for teachers—even though the typical teacher spends as much as a third of his or her professional time engaged in assessment-related activities (Dorr-Bremme & Herman, 1986; Stiggins &

Conklin, 1992). If we really cared about matters of assessment quality, we would have made sure every teacher arrives in the classroom on day one knowing how to dependably assess the achievement of his or her students. We would have made sure every principal has enough assessment literacy to supervise this facet of a teacher's work. Have we done either of these things? We have not. In the future, our assessment systems must arise from a universal foundation of assessment literacy throughout the fabric of American education.

Reason 4: Our Communication of Assessment Results Has Rarely Been Truly Effective.

Although the general public has chosen not to question how well test scores and grades convey information about student achievement, teachers have always struggled with the fact that psychometrically tricky test scores are difficult to interpret, let alone act on, and that we have no universally agreed-upon meaning for letter grades or how to determine them.

The test score version of this communication problem has recently been manifested in the reporting of the results of federally mandated multistate standardized tests developed by a consortium of state departments of education over six years and at a cost of hundreds of millions of dollars. The meaning and instructional relevance of the scores reported remain painfully unclear to their recipients. As we look to the future, our assessments and our communication of assessment results must detail the specific learning targets mastered to date, pointing the way to what must come next in each student's learning.

Reason 5: Until Recently, We Have Not Wanted All Students to Succeed.

Given education's historic mission of sorting students, assessment's traditional role, as we have established, has been to provide the evidence needed to justify this differentiation. The more spread assessment evidence could generate among students, the more dependable would be their rank order at graduation. In effect, over the decades we actually aspired to use assessment to maximize achievement gaps! We created an artificial scarcity of success and made students compete for it, promising winners and losers from the outset.

Teachers motivated students using a reward- and punishment-driven behavior management system. But understand that, in effect, some students were supposed to give up in hopelessness so as to occupy low ranks; it was simply how the system was designed to work. And we accepted it, even though it did harm to many students.

Happily, the new supplementary mission of education—that of promoting universal mastery of lifelong learner proficiencies—means we must redefine the relationships among assessment, student motivation, and student success in ways that sustain a universal belief within all students that "academic success is within my reach if I keep striving for it." While it is unrealistic to hope that all students will attain the same ultimate level of overall academic achievement, it must be our new mission to *help all students acquire the lifelong learning tools needed to reach their potential.* That requires universal motivation to strive for success. We can no longer have any students giving up in hopelessness. We have at our disposal all of the tools and tactics needed to create for our students, ourselves, and our society an inspiring assessment system.

A ROADMAP FOR OUR JOURNEY TO PERFECTION

In this book, I provide detail on the origin and dimensions of our critically important new school mission (Chapter 2), analyze the key components of the perfect assessment system capable of leading to the fulfillment of this new mission (Chapter 3), and dissect each of this system's active ingredients in specific and very practical terms:

- **Assessment purpose**—how to clarify why we assess in truly comprehensive terms (Chapter 4).
- **Learning targets to be assessed**—how to make sure we always know what to assess (Chapter 5).
- **Our definition of assessment quality**—how to do a good job of assessing every time (Chapter 6).
- **Communication of assessment results**—how to share information in ways that serve diverse purposes (Chapter 7).

- **Linking assessment to truly productive *universal* student motivation** (Chapter 8).

Each chapter adds nuance to an understanding of the essential conditions that must be put in place in our schools and classrooms to promote student well-being through excellence in assessment.

With this vision established and the way forward mapped, I summarize the benefits of completing this transformation (Chapter 9), highlighting the good things we can expect for students, their teachers, their supervising school leaders, policymakers, and our parents and communities. *In fact, there are no losers if we navigate this passage successfully—everyone wins!* There are no arguments against making this journey... except, of course, a collective unwillingness to take the risks and make the investments needed to rebuild our assessment infrastructure from scratch. There is no question about how to get there. The only remaining issue is whether we have the will to pay the toll required to make the crossing.

In that regard, this book ends with a summary of the investments we must make. By far, the greatest will be establishing throughout American education that long-missing foundation of assessment literacy—an understanding of the basic principles of sound assessment practice. All who have a stake in the quality of our schools must become assessment literate to a certain degree, including students, teachers, school leaders, policymakers at all levels, and parents and the greater school community. We can no longer remain a nation literally obsessed with raising test scores that understands so little about where these scores come from, what they mean, and what to do with or about them.

We can decide as a society not to make this journey and to cling tenaciously to the dogma of our tired testing traditions. But if that is our choice, we must stop claiming to care about universal student mastery of lifelong learner proficiencies, preparing all students for college and workplace training, achieving educational equity and narrowing achievement gaps, reducing dropout rates, and systematically evaluating school and educator performance in terms of student achievement. None of these crucial social priorities can be achieved given our current assessment culture and the unhealthy educational environment in which assessment is being used. The time has come to stop struggling to make old thinking fit new needs and to move on as quickly as possible to our new assessment future.

In that future, with our perfect assessment system in place, we will gain access to

- Valuable assessment results for all instructional decision makers in all contexts.
- Emphasis on assessment to support learning for each individual student working in collaboration with his or her teacher.
- Clarity of learning targets and agreement on target priorities across contexts, classrooms, schools, districts, and states.
- Continuous and immediate evidence of what comes next in each student's learning.
- Comparable results across contexts and over time.
- Access to the full range of assessment methods in order to reflect even the most complex learning targets.
- Flexible test administration versus universally standardized testing conditions.
- Results that always are easy to interpret and understand versus technical test scores.
- Excellence in communication of results both in formative and summative assessment situations.
- Immediate communication of results versus waiting weeks or months for test scores.
- All students motivated by the belief that academic success is within reach for them if they keep striving for it.

The only way to attain these benefits is to wipe the slate clean and build a completely new assessment infrastructure. A blueprint for doing so follows.

2 A NEW SCHOOL MISSION BRINGS NEW ASSESSMENT DEMANDS

In order to carry on positive action we must develop here a positive vision.

—THE 14TH DALAI LAMA

A good way to understand the diversity of the assessment challenges we face is to consider the range of purposes we want assessment to serve. Think about these examples:

Scenario #1: It is the end of the semester—time for the final exam that will provide information a teacher needs to decide what grade to enter on each student's report card. The teacher reviews the achievement domain—the body of content that has unfolded across the grading period—and outlines the priority topics covered. Then he or she devises assessment exercises and scoring schemes to sample the achievement domain in order to infer what proportion of that required material each student actually mastered. Down the road, of course, the course grade assigned will factor into the determination of each student's cumulative grade point average, which, in turn, will determine each student's rank in class.

Scenario #2: A teacher and student must decide what to tackle next within a particular learning progression. To do so, they need to find out where the student currently stands in that progression. Which of the necessary skills have and have not been mastered? Which understandings have been solidified, and which have not? To answer these questions, the teacher works to transform the learning targets that have been the most recent focus of instruction into assessment exercises and scoring schemes that will reveal the student's current level of proficiency. After the assessment, with the results in front of them, the teacher/student team must infer whether to readdress the recent learning targets or move on to the next ones in the progression.

These two scenarios provide simple but clear illustrations of classroom assessments being used to accomplish two fundamentally different things. To begin with, let's analyze what they have in common. Both assessments have a specific purpose. Both focus on learning targets that students are expected to master. Both use assessment exercises and scoring schemes in order to evaluate student achievement. And because both are intended to inform an instructional decision, they must yield results that are understandable to the decision makers. To be effective, all assessments, in all contexts, must have these characteristics: clear purpose, sharp focus on targets, and clear, dependable results.

What are the differences between the assessments in the preceding scenarios? First, the two scenarios capture different assessment purposes. In Scenario #1, the assessment's purpose is to make a summary judgment regarding the sufficiency of student learning; in Scenario #2, the assessment's purpose is to check learning status in order to figure out how to advance it. Second, the learning targets are different. I don't mean different in terms of subject matter, but different in scope. Scenario #1's assessment is using test items to sample a broad domain of content, while Scenario #2's focus is on a narrower target, probably a single high-priority achievement standard that represents one key step in an unfolding learning progression. These differences in the scope of learning-target focus translate into differences in the assessments: one will include many more exercises than the other. And the nature of the results to be determined, communicated, and acted upon is different too. Scenario #1 will yield a score—the number of items the test-taker got right or the points earned. Scenario #2 will simply support a conclusion—either that the learning target has been mastered or it has not. As we will discuss, these differences exemplify how assessment practices must be adjusted to fit comfortably into the evolving mission of American schools.

Before proceeding, however, I want to add another scenario that presents the same kinds of assessment challenges but in a completely different context:

Scenario #3: A local school district is tasked by the state with conducting an annual accountability test. Once a year, every district in the state is required to conduct this test across several grade levels in order to report school improvement in the form of score changes. The state will also use these scores to compare schools and districts in terms of their demonstrated levels of academic attainment. So the *purpose* of this assessment is to report achievement information to the public and to detect aspects of the curriculum where instruction is strong or in need of strengthening. The *learning targets* in this case are broad domains of content within each subject, often spanning multiple grade levels of that content. Because there are so many students to test and so many tests to score, the most efficient of assessment methods must be used. Most often, this means a multiple-choice test. And because the quality of the test must be very high, this means the state generally uses a published standardized test or contracts with an expert test publisher to construct a version of such a test that is based on the state's chosen academic standards or required curriculum. Numerical scores are reported, and these serve as the basis for all comparative analyses and evaluations.

Any consideration of a new assessment system must accommodate this application of assessment too. Our collective assessment history has included districtwide, statewide, national, and international assessments of this sort. Schools are institutions supported by communities that are entitled to information about the effectiveness of taxpayers' investment.

Later I will fit these scenarios into a comprehensive analysis of the district, school, and classroom contexts that a perfect assessment system must accommodate. But first, let me describe what that system must accomplish for its users.

ASSESSMENT AND THE OLD SCHOOL MISSION

Over the past two decades, our society has expanded the social mission of its schools to include critically important new responsibilities. First, let's establish the depth and strength of the traditional institutional mission and assessment's role in it. Then we can contrast that to the new mission responsibilities so as to understand how and why assessment's role must change.

As mentioned previously, historically, a primary social mission of U.S. schools has been to begin the process of sorting students into the various levels of our social and economic system. We have accomplished this by setting a fixed amount of time to learn (one year per grade level) and allowing the amount learned during that time to vary across students. Some students complete their 1st-grade year having learned a great deal, while others may have learned far less. Those who learned well in 1st grade carry that advantage into 2nd grade and generally continue to grow at the same pace. Those who didn't learn as much in 1st grade tend to lag behind in 2nd grade. Thus, the range of achievement widens by the end of the 2nd-grade year, and it continues to widen year after year as students ascend the grade levels and continue to spread themselves out. The end result is a dependable "rank in class" at the end of high school. The winners come to aspire to college and are driven to continuing success, while at the other end, students who see the evidence of their struggles in the form of their assessment results become frustrated at their chronic failure and give up in hopelessness; about a quarter of them, on average, drop out. Assessment's traditional role has been to provide the evidence of student achievement that underpins this system.

There is an underlying motivational belief at work here. Society and its educators have believed that by limiting opportunities for ultimate success, they can create a competitive environment that will drive students to strive for more learning. This belief holds that those who have achieved a high level will strive to remain on top and those ranked lower than they want to be will work harder to improve their grades and attain ever-higher positions in the pecking order. This belief also holds that those who suffer from chronic failure and achieve very low rankings must just not care or "don't want to work hard." When they drop out, it means limited resources can be redirected to those who are willing and able to learn.

Standardized achievement tests that emerged in the middle of the past century and remain in place today were, and are, designed to fit into this institutional sorting routine. They are specifically and intentionally designed to detect differences in student achievement. The test developers outline very broad achievement domains as their learning targets and create multiple-choice test items to sample that content. The test items are pilot tested, and those deemed to be of the highest quality are selected to appear on the final form of the test. Quality criteria for test items' selection include a test item's ability to detect differences in student mastery of the content covered (i.e., these items are the best possible discriminators or differentiators). When final test assembly is complete, the test is technically capable of differentiating among respondents' mastery of the domain all the way from the highest scorer to the lowest. This provides the basis for what is known as *norm-referenced test score interpretation*.

College admissions tests are classic examples. They are designed to identify those who have attained the highest levels of achievement in the domains sampled among college applicants, and these tests perform this service well. Over the past half-century, test developers have created and marketed these kinds of standardized tests all the way down into the primary grades.

Historically, report card grading practices followed this same value proposition. The earliest versions were called "grading on a curve," in which teachers began instruction having decided that only a few top students would receive an *A*, a few more would receive a *B*, and so on. The purpose of grades was to support the institutional mission of sorting the most able learners from the least able ones.

While this kind of rigid grading system has been abandoned in most contexts, an echo of it remains today. Many educators and members of our school communities assume that if a teacher assigns too many high report card grades, this represents evidence that the curriculum lacks rigor. It means that the teacher is contributing to "grade inflation"—a bad thing, deemed to be degrading the quality of our schools. Grades, they contend, should serve to spread students along a continuum of achievement.

BUT NOW, A NEW SCHOOL MISSION...

The accelerating social and technical evolution of our culture over the first two decades of the 21st century has made us aware that our schools need to do far more than sort students. By the turn of the century, it had become obvious that our schools must provide all students with the lifelong learner proficiencies that will allow them to keep up with the rapid pace of change. The problem, we realized, is that those who finish low in the rank order or drop out under the old mission of schools fail to develop essential lifelong learner proficiencies—foundational literacy and numeracy as well as the key reasoning and problem-solving skills they need to survive in our culture and contribute to its ongoing development. From now on, we decided, schools should "leave no child behind" in this regard.

So schools have been assigned an additional responsibility: to make sure "every student succeeds" at mastering fundamental reading, writing, mathematics, problem solving, and other proficiencies that they will need in this increasingly complex and fast-changing world. Political forums and media outlets herald the new mission almost daily: *all students are to be made ready for college and the workplace.* In effect, schools have been charged with addressing the reality that our economy has great difficulty absorbing those who fail to finish high school without the tools they need to move on to post-secondary training.

And so, society has directed that the chronic achievement gaps that have separated subgroups of our student population for decades must be narrowed. Persistently high dropout rates must be reduced. Note, however, that this new social mission does not absolve educators from delivering a dependable rank order based on achievement at the end of high school. It's just that the revised sorting process begins and goes upward from "competent lifelong learner."

If we are to fulfill an expanded mission that now includes universal academic success in certain achievement arenas, then our assessments must deliver far more than evidence for grading, sorting, and weeding out. They must also become teaching tools—tools that motivate all students and promote maximum success for all.

WEAVING ASSESSMENT INTO A NEW SCHOOL MISSION

Please reflect briefly on the scenarios that opened this chapter in light of this expanded mission and role for assessment. Two of them fit into a "sort and select" purpose for assessment; the other (Scenario #2) centered on the use of assessment to support student learning rather than to merely measure and document it. This highlights one of the trickiest challenges we face in achieving our new school mission: creating assessments that can be used both to support learning, when that is the purpose, and to judge the sufficiency of learning, when that is appropriate.

Remember also that the assessments in Scenarios #1 and #3 sampled a wide domain of achievement, while the one in Scenario #2 focused on a single, high-priority learning target. The key lessons to be learned here? First, when assessment is used to support learning, we need to define our learning targets—what we identify as important for students to master—with great precision. Second, we need to clearly and appropriately articulate the individual proficiencies, competencies, or achievement standards to be taught and assessed, and we need to make these articulations public for all to see.

Further, because high-stakes accountability tests have carried such weight and had such high visibility over recent decades, practically all concern about and resource allocations for test quality have been focused on them. However, as we begin to count more and more on classroom assessments—both to support learning and to judge and certify it—matters of assessment quality become critically important here too. Ensuring appropriate levels of assessment literacy for all assessment users at all levels of use places a burden on local school districts to provide any needed professional development. I will return to this issue toward the end of the chapter.

Next, as we transition to assessment for the expanded school mission, we must address the communication of assessment results. Obviously, a single set of annual test scores will not meet teachers' classroom-level information needs. To support learning, teachers need assessment results that describe the current state of student learning and help to reveal what should come next in that learning. Gross domain sample test scores alone won't help learners much either. To figure out how to do better next time, students need feedback that contains more specific information than they're currently receiving.

In an encouraging development, the College Board has manifested a keen awareness of our changing school mission in its recent transformation of the traditional SAT college admission examination into an assessment and reporting system that provides teachers and students with diagnostic information on student needs for instructional planning (College Board, 2015). The standard Math and Verbal scores have been replaced by an array of 15 scores linked to instructional pathways to help students promote their own college readiness. In terms of the totally balanced assessment system to which we aspire, the transformation of one summary annual test is a small step, but it is an important one.

Finally, to accommodate this multifaceted mission for our schools, we need to reconceptualize the relationship between assessment and student motivation. Now that teachers must motivate *all* students to strive for lifelong learner competence (rather than just a few at the top of the rank order), the old way—demanding high performance and threatening dire consequences for failure in order to drive up student anxiety—will not do the job. The traditional value proposition underpinning assessment and student motivation, built on creating an artificial scarcity of academic success and asking students to compete for it and prove themselves to be "winners" or "losers," is no longer tenable in a society that cannot afford any losers.

If we seek to narrow achievement gaps and reduce dropout rates, we can no longer have any students giving up in hopelessness. When it comes to the development of reading, writing, mathematical problem solving, critical thinking, and other lifelong learning skills, we need and we must seek to have nothing but winners. To get all students to work hard, we must offer them all a promising future, in concrete and specific terms, that they believe is within reach for them. Our assessment system must become a mirror in which they can watch themselves coming ever closer to the levels of competence they need to attain that future. In other words, we must motivate with self-directed learning success rather than the intimidation and anxiety of accountability.

ASSESSMENT LITERACY IS THE FOUNDATION

As we reexamine the relationship between assessment and truly effective schools in light of our educational system's new aspirations, it becomes clear that whatever we do in pursuit of perfection must rely on high-quality assessments effectively used to promote student learning success. Regardless of context, all assessments must do the following:

- Arise from and serve a pre-set, clear, and appropriate purpose.
- Arise from and accurately reflect a clear and appropriate learning target.
- Rely on high-quality exercises and scoring schemes to yield dependable evidence.
- Communicate results effectively to the intended user of results.
- Link productively to the dynamics of student motivation.

Within the measurement community, these are universally endorsed standards of sound assessment practice, and they are not negotiable. All who wish to build or use sound assessments must attain and apply some level of understanding of these standards. The depth of that understanding—that is, the required level of assessment literacy—will vary depending on the extent and nature of the user's involvement with assessment. Here is my ranking of the populations most in need of assessment literacy, beginning with those who require the highest level:

1. Professional test developers. These assessors must develop the deepest levels of understanding of sound practice, including how to create and defend high-quality assessments that fit into pre-established contexts of purpose and learning target, and how to communicate results in the form of useful information on which practitioners can act productively.

2. State and local district assessment directors. This level of involvement in assessment practice may include assessment development as described above, requiring a strong technical background in testing methodology. But perhaps more important is these directors' mastery of the ability to translate complex measurement concepts into commonsense ideas that can be discussed with practitioners, using everyday language, in the service of promoting the assessment literacy of those teachers and school leaders.

3. Teachers and local school leaders. As already mentioned, teachers spend a sizeable portion of their professional time engaged in assessment-related activities. Assessment represents a major part of their job, and student well-being hinges on them doing it well. Indeed, the professional well-being of teachers themselves often depends on the quality of the evidence of student learning that's being used to evaluate their instruction. Teachers' supervisors must be sufficiently assessment literate to help teachers gather and use dependable evidence to support and to certify learning.

4. Policymakers. This group includes federal, state, and local policymakers; state department of education personnel; and members of professional organizations who seek to influence policy. Because policy guides practice, we need the best possible assessment policies at all levels. Obviously, to set sound policies, these leaders must bring to the process an appropriate level of assessment literacy.

5. Parents and the school community in general. They are charged with protecting the assessment rights of their families and children. To successfully carry out this duty, they must understand the differences between sound and unsound assessment practices and the rights in need of protection.

It's frightening to anticipate what it would mean if any one of these groups lacked the assessment literacy needed to fulfill their particular responsibilities. What if, for example, teachers and school leaders had not been given the opportunity to master the principles of sound assessment practice?

They would be unable to link assessment effectively to teaching and learning, unable to provide leadership in managing this facet of instruction, incapable of setting sound assessment policies, and powerless to protect their children from assessment harm.

Well, as alarming as this potential problem is to acknowledge, the fact is that professional educators (teachers and administrators) typically *do not* receive preservice or inservice training in classroom assessment. That leaves local, state, and federal policymakers, as well as parents and communities, with nowhere to turn for help in understanding key assessment issues and vulnerable to persuasion by test publishers pursuing commercial interests. Unless this regrettable cycle of assessment illiteracy is broken, the assessment quagmire we find ourselves in will continue to deepen. The perfect assessment system I envision is built on a foundation of understanding of the basic principles of sound assessment practice.

3 OVERVIEW OF THE PERFECT ASSESSMENT CULTURE AND SYSTEM

Perfection is not attainable, but if we chase perfection we can catch excellence.

—VINCE LOMBARDI

This chapter begins our look at how we can break from outmoded assessment traditions. I introduce the values propositions and the assessment culture needed to frame, organize, and make operational a truly productive alternative to current practices—*the perfect assessment system.* I offer the vision for this system in five parts that correspond to the five keys to sound assessment practice identified in Chapter 1:

- Clear assessment purposes
- Clear learning targets
- High-quality assessment
- Effective communication of results
- Powerful new links to student motivation

You'll read more about each of these five keys in the chapters ahead, but I believe it's valuable to present the total integrated vision before we get into the details of how we might achieve it.

THE MATTER OF PURPOSE

When it comes to recreating assessment culture in our schools, the key is to *balance* our uses of assessment to serve all relevant purposes (users and uses). We have been so far out of assessment balance for so long that overall school quality has suffered as a result. After introducing the balanced assessment concept as part of this initial picture, I'll fill in specific details in Chapter 4.

As already stipulated, assessment is the process of gathering evidence of student achievement to inform instructional decisions. Sometimes decision makers can use assessment to help students learn more, and at other times they can use it to evaluate and report the sufficiency of learning in relation to expectations. The list of assessment users is long, as is the number of decisions that assessment results can inform.

When thinking of assessment in systems terms, it is important to understand that these different users need different kinds of information in different forms and at different times to do their jobs. Clearly, no single assessment can serve them all, and yet over the past decades we have allocated our assessment resources as if one could. So heavily have we invested in meeting the information needs of those who use annual assessment for accountability that there's been little left to meet the needs of other truly important decision makers, such as those who are interested in using assessment to support learning on an ongoing basis in schools and classrooms. The result has been a gross imbalance.

Assessment results are used in three distinct contexts within the educational process. All three are critical to student well-being. Teachers, students, and their parents rely on evidence gathered using continuous *classroom assessment*. In addition, teacher teams and instructional leaders sometimes rely on periodic or *interim benchmark assessments* to track changes in student achievement. And finally, school and district leaders, as well as policymakers, rely on evidence gathered using *annual accountability tests*. Assessment results in these three contexts all serve important purposes, but those purposes are different.

Over the decades, we have invested so much in ensuring the quality of annual standardized tests that we have left the quality of classroom and interim assessments almost completely unaddressed. Do teachers, students, parents, teacher teams, and instructional leaders have the dependable assessment evidence they need to make decisions that support student learning and well-being? We don't know, and neither do they.

But imbalance has not stopped there. We have established that practitioners can use assessments for two general purposes: to support student learning (formative applications) and to evaluate the sufficiency of that learning (summative assessment). Both are important, but they are different too. Here again, one of the purposes has dominated the other, and it's the latter one: use of results to make summative judgments about the amount students have learned. Traditionally, assessments have not been seen or used as tools to promote learning, and this perspective has contributed to our heavy focus on annual standardized tests. For many in our policy-setting communities, these tests have come to be seen as the universal key to school improvement: *Just hold educators accountable for raising scores,* they contend, *and then everything will improve.*

In fact, there is little research evidence to defend this belief (Amrein & Berliner, 2002; Wiliam, 2010). However, it is safe to assume that annual accountability tests help us identify achievement problems and provide the means for public disclosure, even if they do little to help fix those problems. For assessments that are effective fixers, far better bets are classroom and interim benchmark assessments. When it comes to improving learning, the most impactful decision makers are not at the state or federal level but at the local school district level, in schools and classrooms. Topping the list of key users are the teachers *and their students* who use day-to-day classroom assessment to support individual breakthroughs. It has not been our convention to include students in our list of assessment users. But, as it turns out, they pay attention to the evidence of their own learning success and make crucial decisions based on their interpretation of their own assessment results. These decisions can have long-lasting consequences.

As we look to the future, the assessment spotlight must expand to include assessment designed to inform local instructional decisions that promote student growth and create a balanced system to meet the needs of all summative *and* formative assessment users.

I can see only one way to build a system that can bring maximum assistance to districts, schools, teachers, and students while also providing for institutional accountability. It is outlined in the sections that follow. It is my fervent hope that policymakers and practitioners at all levels will permit and support (or at least not prohibit) the development of such a culture. In fact, if they have any hope of using assessment productively to promote student well-being, I think they have no choice.

THE MATTER OF LEARNING TARGETS

When it comes to defining achievement expectations to underpin assessments capable of informing instructional decisions, the watchword is *precision*. Historically, we have relied on assessment to give us gross test scores representative of student achievement in broad but very shallow content domains. As a result, while assessment scores have served accountability purposes, their imprecision has rendered them instructionally impotent. To counter this, we need assessments that focus much more sharply on individual learning targets. The perfect assessment system described herein does this by putting the assessment spotlight on individual, high-priority achievement standards and not on broad domains of standards or content.

Learning targets or achievement standards form the foundation of any assessment. They dictate what will be reflected in test items, exercises or tasks, and scoring guidelines. The items on a large-scale annual accountability test may sample a year's worth of content or sometimes even more. They yield evidence (scores) that can support dependable inferences about whether or not students have mastered all the material included in very broad content domains. While this kind of evidence is useful for school leaders who are required to report gains or deficiencies in literacy or mathematics achievement across and among student populations, by and large, it does nothing to inform the kinds of decisions teachers and students make in the classroom to advance student growth along relevant learning progressions. A once-a-year set of scores with no clear connection to specific skills, competencies, or learning progressions is useless when deciding what to do on a day-to-day basis to promote learning.

In a perfect assessment system, long dominant domain-referenced thinking gives way to *standards-referenced thinking* (or, alternatively, *competence-referenced thinking*). The only way to secure the precise, instructionally actionable results educators need is to assess each individual standard or competency so that we can see which targets need instructional intervention. This expands assessment's role from identifying achievement problems to helping to solve those problems. Such standards-referenced evidence can inform instructional decisions focused on individual student success, and it can be aggregated across students at classroom, school, and district levels to inform decisions with broader reach, including judgments of the sufficiency of learning for accountability purposes. No one's information needs have to go unmet. In Chapter 5, I will explain how this can be accomplished.

THE MATTER OF ASSESSMENT QUALITY

Student mastery of any standard can only be detected using *high-quality assessments* regardless of context—state, local district, school, or classroom. When we are confident that each assessment of each standard meets accepted quality benchmarks, irrespective of where that assessment was developed or by whom, then we can count on different assessments of the same standard to yield dependable and comparable inferences about student mastery of the standard in question. With evidence of this quality and comparability arising from classrooms, schools, and districts, *standardized tests as we have known them are no longer necessary*. We don't need all students across all schools or districts throughout the state to respond to exactly the same set of test items at the same time under identical conditions.

In the perfect system, these inferences about student mastery of each specific standard question are the only ones that matter. When looking at individual students, we ask, "Did this student demonstrate mastery of this standard or not?" When looking at whole classrooms and the school, we ask, "What proportion of students mastered this standard? Who did and who didn't?" As you can see, the inferences this system allows can easily support formative decisions about what comes next in the learning for individual students or groups of students as well as summative decisions about overall school effectiveness when the scores are aggregated across classrooms, schools, districts, and other student subgroups.

To ensure all assessments are high-quality assessments, the criteria must be clear and universally acknowledged, understood, and applied. A high-quality assessment does the following:

- Relies on an appropriate assessment method given the learning target in question.
- Collects a sufficient sample of student performance to support the desired inference without wasting time gathering too much evidence.
- Uses assessment exercise and scoring schemes that align directly with the target in question and that meet accepted standards of quality.
- Minimizes bias that can distort its results.

Assessment-literate practitioners understand and commit to meeting these standards of quality; therefore, one of the pillars of a perfect assessment system is a universal foundation of assessment literacy. Everyone involved in collecting evidence of standards mastery must understand and be able to apply basic principles of sound assessment.

When this universal foundation of assessment competence is in place, then high-quality tests can come from a wide variety of sources. State departments of education will be free to develop standards-based achievement assessments and disseminate these for local use, or local districts can develop their own if they wish. Indeed, schools and teachers can develop their own assessments, as long as this work meets accepted standards of test quality.

States or local districts might create libraries of these assessments to be accessed by educators at all levels for formative or summative uses. Each test entered into such a bank would need to specify the standard assessed, provide instructions for use, and include test exercises and scoring guidelines as well as a written description of how that assessment satisfies validity, reliability, and fairness standards. This last piece would defend the assessment method used given the learning target, the sufficiency and quality of the sample collected, the equality of the exercises and scoring schemes, and how potential sources of bias have been identified and addressed.

Assessments created in this manner can be used strategically during the school year to support student learning or whenever instruction on a particular standard has been completed to document student mastery. Again, there's no longer any need to administer a one-time standardized state or districtwide annual test.

Some will argue that practitioners do not currently possess the assessment literacy necessary to pull this off. This is true, and has been for decades. But aren't we then compelled to ask whether there are other routine classroom assessment applications that some (perhaps many) practitioners are also insufficiently assessment literate to carry out? If the answer to that question is yes (and I think it is), then many teachers may be troublingly unprepared to weave assessment into instruction. We cannot remain where we are now, which is instructionally impaired by a lack of assessment literacy, and we cannot move to the new vision of instructionally useful assessment for the same reason. I think this problem suggests its own solution, and it's something we will explore in Chapter 6.

THE MATTER OF EFFECTIVE COMMUNICATION

With educational aspirations centered on maximizing learning, we can no longer rely on confusing test scores ("data") that are reflective of student mastery of broad content domains. We can't ask teacher "data teams" to ferret out the meaning of truly complex and confusing test score evidence when they are neither trained nor qualified to do so. Rather, we must develop ways of sharing assessment results that give teachers *immediately useable information* about students' mastery of each standard, thus removing all manner of confusion about evidence of success. With this model, we know students are succeeding when we see that each student's list of "standards mastered" is growing, and we know that schools are effective when we see that the proportion of students demonstrating mastery of the highest-priority achievement standards is increasing. Our perfect assessment system allows us to capture and convey this information accurately and easily.

As noted, in the perfect system, every assessment we use, regardless of who created it or the context we're using it in, dependably reflects student mastery of clear and appropriate learning targets. This dramatically simplifies record-keeping requirements and the procedures for communicating results. We can keep records for individual students that report which standards each student has mastered, and because those records can be easily aggregated across students as the percent mastering each standard, we can report results by classroom, school, or district, as well as by any desired subgroup of students. State results can logically center on the previously agreed-upon statewide standards, while districts, schools, or classrooms that have added their own targets can track and report on their unique standards. In short, in a perfect assessment system, percentages can be aggregated or disaggregated, as desired, for both public reporting and instructional decision making.

Local districts, schools, or teachers can use this kind of assessment (whether the test is theirs, the state's, or from a test publisher) in a pre-test/post-test manner to examine or support student growth over whatever time span they choose. Teachers can use standard-focused evidence to remain in constant touch with each student's current place in the progression of standards so they and their students can figure out what should come next in the learning and fine-tune its pace. In Chapter 7, I will describe the essence of the formative and summative record keeping and communication systems to be developed.

LINKING ASSESSMENT TO STUDENT MOTIVATION

The link between assessment and motivation goes to the very essence of why we assess. Historically, we have assessed to generate evidence to reward learning success, thus helping the successful finish high in the rank order of achievement. But, as we have established, casting assessment in this role gives it the power to punish the lack of learning success, potentially dooming some students to what they believe to be inevitable failure and building in them a sense of hopelessness that prevents them from mastering essential lifelong learner proficiencies. The new assessment culture we need will address this dilemma in a number of ways.

Perhaps the most important key to motivating students to strive for academic success is to make sure they believe success is within reach for them if they keep trying. Generally speaking, this confidence is available only to those who actually are succeeding. If students tumble into a losing streak and lose faith in themselves as learners, chances are they will never regain that faith. Young children who once loved to learn become focused on getting right answers instead of wrong ones; those with a history of struggle are in constant danger of giving up. While this once was acceptable—and indeed, was part of the design of schools—it no longer fits into the new and expanded mission we have set.

The perfect assessment system puts in place a variety of safeguards against these eventualities. It features ways to help students remain confident, engaged, and seeking the learning versus intimidated, anxious, and seeking the grade. We must remain mindful of the importance of these emotional dynamics given the new mission of schools and educators' accountability for narrowing achievement gaps, reducing dropout rates, and delivering universal lifelong learner competence.

It is time to stop thinking of assessment merely as something adults do to students. Yes, it is one of our responsibilities as educators, and we must do it well. But we can't forget that students judge their own achievement as well. They, too, use their assessment results as the basis for critical decisions. Through their analysis of their own academic record, they decide whether they have hope of success, whether the risk of future failure outweighs the benefits of trying or not, and whether to invest the energy needed to succeed. When students come down on the wrong side of these decisions, it doesn't matter what the adults around them decide to do: the learning just stops.

The perfect system envisioned herein helps to maintain each student's sense of academic self-efficacy and willingness to continue learning, and it does this by helping all students

- Become key players in a self-assessment process as they learn and rely on that involvement to promote their own success.
- Stay aware of where they are within whatever learning progression they are ascending and of what comes next for them.
- Use continuous evidence of changes in their own levels of mastery to monitor and feel in control of their growth over time.

Clearly, this is not the classroom assessment system most of us grew up in. In this new system, during the learning, teachers and their students are partners in the pursuit of ongoing academic success. Students aren't left to guess about learning targets; these are always clear to all involved, as are the pathways to success. As they learn, students share responsibility for both promoting and providing evidence of their own growth. Teachers are responsible for getting students on winning streaks and keeping them there. Research conducted around the world over the past two decades tells us that when these realities play out for students and their teachers, achievement skyrockets. I will discuss why in Chapter 6.

THE NEW VISION IN A NUTSHELL

As we examine our vision of the perfect assessment system, we see concrete and specific ways to use assessment to meet the information needs of all assessment users, from the classroom to the boardroom, as they endeavor both to support and to certify student learning. In this ideal future, teachers, school leaders, and policymakers are as clear about what students are striving to learn as students themselves are. Assessments always yield dependable evidence of each student's current level of attainment in each of the identified standards' learning progressions, thus keeping all students and their teachers continuously informed about what comes next in the learning. Those assessment results are always communicated to intended users in a timely and understandable manner. And all students strive for academic excellence because they believe it is valuable and achievable for them.

ASSESSMENTS THAT SERVE *ALL* USERS AND USES

It is not unreasonable to believe that the educational significance of locally produced tests may far outweigh that of the occasional standardized test.

—ROBERT L. EBEL

If assessment is about gathering information to inform instructional decisions, then one cannot begin the assessment process in any particular context without answers to three essential questions in that context:

- What is the decision to be made?
- Who will make that decision?
- What information will they need to make a good decision?

All three of these questions speak to assessment purpose. Without answers to these questions, how do we know what knowledge or skills to reflect in the assessment's exercises and scoring schemes? How do we decide on the form of the results, to whom they should be delivered, or when to deliver them? Unless we can definitively identify the assessment decision to be made, the decision maker, and the information required to make that decision, we have no business creating, choosing, or administering either large-scale tests or classroom ones. When it comes to effective assessment, purpose is everything.

To promote a culture of student learning success, we have established that a wide variety of decision makers are charged with responsibility for making a wide array of really important instructional decisions. Some decisions are made day to day in the classroom, based on evidence derived from continuous *classroom assessment*; others require more *periodic assessments* to track progress, and still others must be *annual tests* used to check and report achievement status.

ASSESSMENT ASSUMPTIONS AND THE UNDERLYING REALITIES

Since the 1950s, U.S. federal and state legislation has typically conceived of assessment as annual accountability testing used to provide evidence of student mastery of achievement expectations in the broad achievement domains of language arts, math, and science, among others. These tests are expected to meet standards of quality, sampling the prescribed content domains with large numbers of test items and generating valid and reliable results. Qualified content experts establish cutoff scores that serve as the basis for judgments about whether the examinees have mastered the learning targets that make up the domain. Evidence is gathered from all students throughout a certain range of grades. Results are designed to be aggregated and disaggregated according to the several categories of students and to be comparable across classrooms, schools, and districts. The results are delivered to policymakers and school leaders, who use them to drive school improvement efforts. The purposes these assessments are intended to serve are numerous and diverse:

- To evaluate schools for public accountability reporting.
- To compare student scores across subpopulations and contexts.
- To identify and describe student academic needs so as to inform instruction.
- To inform parents and the community of schools' resource needs.

Over the decades, problems have persisted with this iconic vision of testing. One of the most prominent has been uncertainty over sampling. Which particular learning targets or achievement standards are actually included in a particular test, which are not, and why? Because of this uncertainty, assessment users cannot rely on test results to indicate which of the standards has been mastered by which students. So it is difficult to interpret the educational meaning or implications of resulting scores or to link gross test scores to actions that are likely to result in better teaching and learning.

I'm about to briefly recount the history of this vision of excellence in assessment, and as I do, allow a mental cash register to ring up the accumulating probable costs of standardized testing over the decades. Please understand that my objective is *not* to discount the decision-informing value of accountability testing, something that I am in favor of under the right circumstances. Rather, I believe that a clear sense of this history can teach us important lessons regarding the specific conditions that must be satisfied for assessment to actually contribute to the improvement of our schools.

In the United States, our belief in the power of accountability testing to improve schools

- Began with districtwide testing in the 1950s.
- Led to states being ranked in the media based on their average college admissions test score in the 1960s.
- Caused us to add statewide testing in the 1970s.
- Continued the march with national assessment in the 1970s and 1980s.
- Advanced to international assessment in the 1990s.
- Embraced every-pupil No Child Left Behind testing in the new millennium.
- "Raced to the top" in the 2010s with tests from the Smarter Balanced Assessment Consortium and the Partnership for Assessment of Readiness for College and Careers (PARCC).

Virtually all of these levels of testing remain in place today in some form and at a cost of billions of dollars over the decades. Is it any wonder there's so much consternation over too much testing?

In light of this costly expansion of accountability testing, consider this: In a synthesis of investigations of the impact of accountability testing on student achievement, Wiliam (2010) reports results ranging from no impact whatsoever (e.g., Amrein & Berliner, 2002) to effect sizes of a small fraction

of a standard deviation (several studies reviewed) in which effects were miti-
gated by undesirable unintended side effects such as a narrowing of the curriculum, demoralized teachers, and undue pressure on students (e.g., Cizek,
2005). The key lesson here is that we must keep the potential contribution
of accountability tests to student learning in perspective. It's impossible for
any once-a-year accountability test to serve all of the assessment purposes
typically asked of it in authorizing legislation. Such tests are simply too infre-
quent and superficial to inform the instructional decisions that drive teaching
and learning or school quality.

By contrast, there is an extensive international body of rigorous research
demonstrating the contribution that day-to-day classroom assessments make
to improved student learning. In this case, gains in student achievement of
half to three-quarters of a standard deviation or more are reported (see Black
& Wiliam, 1998a, 1998b; Hattie & Timperley, 2007). This is good news in
the sense that we don't need to rely on annual testing to do a job for which
it's ill-suited; it represents just one part of what can be a total vision of assessment for student success. But it's bad news in the sense that our historical,
bordering on obsessive, focus on accountability testing as the answer to
school improvement has led us to overlook just how critical classroom assessment can be—and how dire the consequences of poor classroom assessment
can be for learners. If teachers are gathering inaccurate evidence of student
achievement and, thus, making incorrect instructional decisions, interven-
tions based on interim or annual assessment data cannot undo this damage.

The foundation of a truly effective assessment system really is the classroom level of assessment. If it is working well, then and only then can
accountability and interim testing make their contributions. Unfortunately,
we have been overlooking this truth for decades, beginning with the federal
Elementary and Secondary Education Act in 1965 and its assumption that
high-stakes annual standardized tests would fix any problems. This oversight
has been naïve at best and immensely harmful to student well-being at worst.
A perfect assessment system corrects this error, and it does so by relying on
classroom, interim, and annual assessment to help practitioners make three
major categories of instructional decisions.

We've talked some about the first two decision categories—the way that assessment can (1) help teachers judge and evaluate the sufficiency of learning and (2) inform teachers about how to support student learning. These, we have established, are what we refer to as *summative* and *formative* applications of assessment. The third category is a special application of formative classroom assessment called *assessment FOR learning* that involves students in ongoing self-assessment as they grow, to keep them seeing and feeling in control of their progress. This increases their chances of ultimate success. In my work, I have separated out this special formative application because, while I have had no difficulty helping teachers embrace the formative idea, entertaining a role for students to play in the assessment process has been out of reach for many. It is in its own category to bring attention to this powerful new play within the assessment realm.

In assessment FOR learning, students become instructional decision makers, collaborating with their teachers in deciding what actions to take on the basis of their interpretation of their own results. A perfect assessment system informs all of these users and uses with dependable evidence upon which they can base decisions for promoting learning progress and student success. Anything short of this is unacceptable.

Figure 1 provides a more detailed analysis of the active ingredients of a truly balanced local school district assessment system in terms of classroom, interim, and annual assessments that serve formative and summative assessment purposes. It identifies the decision makers, the key instructional decisions they must make, and the information they need to do their jobs. *We build balanced, instructionally helpful assessment systems only when we honor the information needs of all instructional decision makers identified in this table.*

Make special note of the consistency in the kinds of information needed across assessment contexts. In all cases, *key decisions require evidence of which specific individual achievement standards have and have not been mastered.* As students ascend learning progressions to ever-higher levels of achievement, they climb on standards already mastered to reach the next standards in the progression. I will analyze this key to productive assessment further in Chapter 5's look at learning targets.

FIGURE 1
Instructional Decision Framework Addressed in a Balanced Assessment System

CLASSROOM ASSESSMENT	Formative Applications—Diagnostic	Formative Applications—Assessment FOR Learning	Summative Applications
Key decision maker(s):	Teacher	Student/teacher team	Teacher
Important instructional decisions to be made:	"What comes next in my students' learning?"	"What comes next in my learning? Can I master it?"	"What grade or standards mastered go on report cards?"
Information needed to inform decisions:	Standards collected into clear and appropriate learning progressions Evidence of standards mastered and not yet and types of problems students are having	Student-friendly standards-based learning progressions Diagnostic evidence of each student's current place in learning progressions and of any problems students are having	Evidence of student mastery of each required standard

PERIODIC BENCHMARK TESTS	Formative Applications—Diagnostic	Formative Applications—Assessment FOR Learning	Summative Applications
Key decision maker(s):	Curriculum and instructional leaders, teacher teams, professional learning communities	Teachers, but students can assist in interpreting assessment results	Curriculum and instructional leaders
Important instructional decisions to be made:	"Which standards are our students struggling to master, and what can we do about it?"	"Which standards do my students (or do I, the student) struggle to master, and why?"	"Which standards are large numbers of our students not mastering?"
Information needed to inform decisions:	Evidence of standards covered but not mastered by all or most students	Evidence of standards my students have failed to master	Evidence of standards mastered or not across classrooms or school based on common assessments

FIGURE 1

Instructional Decision Framework Addressed in a Balanced Assessment System–*(continued)*

ANNUAL TESTS	Formative Applications– Diagnostic	Formative Applications– Assessment FOR Learning	Summative Applications
Key decision maker(s):	Curriculum and instructional leaders		District leadership team, school board, and community
Important instructional decisions to be made:	"What required standards* did our students not master?" *Results must reveal how each student has done in mastering each standard.*	*There is no assessment FOR learning application of annual tests.*	"Did enough of our students master required standards*?" *Results must reveal how each student has done in mastering each standard*
Information needed to inform decisions:	Evidence of required (expected) standards mastered or not		Evidence of the proportion of our students mastering each standard

Source: From *Assessment Balance and Quality: An Action Guide for School Leaders* (pp. 14–15), by S. Chappuis, C. Commodore, and R. Stiggins, 2010, Columbus, OH: Pearson Education. Copyright 2010 by S. Chappuis, C. Commodore, and R. Stiggins. Adapted with permission.

Note also the dimensionality of the decision-making framework. Now our long-standing belief in summative assessment's ability to improve schools by evaluating and certifying learning is accompanied by two other formative applications that use assessment to guide and support learning. *The power of assessment to improve school quality and student success is increased exponentially by using it not just to measure the effects of teaching but also to literally cause learning.*

Look again in Figure 1 at the role students play in this new vision of the assessment process. For decades, we have treated assessment as adult work. Our policies and practices have reflected the belief that, if we could just get the right information into the hands of the right adult decision makers, then, as if by magic, schools would improve dramatically. This is precisely what the progression I described earlier—standardized testing's expansion from districtwide to statewide to national to international—has been about. I submit that part of the reason for the lack of impact of this progression is that it leaves out a major player in the instructional decision-making team: students.

In the "Assessment FOR Learning" column of Figure 1, the questions for students are "What comes next in my learning?" and "Can I master it?" The second of these may be the most important question in the entire chart. If any student's answer, based on a personal analysis and interpretation of his or her academic record, is "No, I can't," then every other instructional decision becomes meaningless. The learning stops. The perfect assessment system prevents this through the consistent application of principles of assessment FOR learning. It helps students to always know where they are headed, where they are now in relation to those expectations, and how to close the gap between those two points. I will discuss precisely how in Chapter 8's look at the way that our perfect system links assessment and student motivation.

For an example of how this kind of multidimensional thinking about assessment's role is influencing school improvement policy, I would point readers to *A New Path for Oregon System of Assessment to Empower Meaningful Student Learning* (Oregon Education Association, Oregon Department of Education, & Oregon Education Investment Board, 2015). Created by a team of teachers, school leaders from local districts, and the governor's office, it's a model of assertive leadership for productive change.

A SUMMARY OF PURPOSEFUL ASSESSMENT

In its essence, a perfect assessment system honors the information needs of each of these key decision makers. Ultimate student success hinges on each of the key decisions being made well. Ineffective decision making at any level can slow or stop the learning. In other words, all relevant assessment purposes must be effectively served.

Historically, this standard of educational excellence simply has not been met. As detailed earlier, virtually all of our assessment policies, resources, and societal attention have centered on the "Summative Applications" column.

And virtually all of those have been devoted to the annual accountability assessment cell of that column. Yet it is the other cells of Figure 1 that promise to drive school quality and student learning success. Twenty years of international research backs this assertion. The perfect system at the district level values all of the cells and fills them with the resources needed to ensure and support the development of truly effective schools. We can have public school accountability and quality assessment in all contexts only if we balance the information needs of all users.

5 START WITH CLEAR AND APPROPRIATE LEARNING TARGETS

Arriving at one goal is the starting point to another.

—JOHN DEWEY

In addition to starting the assessment process with a clear sense of *why* we are assessing (including who will use results and how), we must also always start with a clear vision of *what* is to be assessed. The achievement expectations, standards, proficiencies, competencies, learning outcomes, and instructional goals and objectives (pick the label you prefer) we establish represent the knowledge, reasoning, skills, and values we want our schools to instill. They form our academic culture. Our children will build upon these foundational school learnings throughout the rest of their learning lives.

The most important breakthrough in assessment of the 21st century is that we now understand how to use assessments *both* to help students master instructional goals and to certify this mastery. Our learning targets define what our assessments will assess in the service of these agendas. First we articulate the desired targets, and then we transform these targets into assessment exercises and scoring procedures.

As we look back at our assessment history, often it appears that we have had this assessment thinking backward, and we are dealing with the consequences. In the case of large-scale standardized testing, the logistical demands of mass testing have had a strong impact on what gets tested. Faced with the need to assess hundreds of thousands of students statewide, the only economically feasible method is a machine-scored, multiple-choice test, meaning that the only targets that can be tested are those that can be translated into that format. Learning targets that don't translate into multiple-choice items are excluded and, thus, become less valued in our school curriculum.

In the perfect assessment system, this does not happen. We can align the testing method to whatever targets we value. Targets that require the use of written assessment, performance assessment, or detailed personal interaction are no longer excluded.

As a specialist in education assessment and not curriculum, I am unqualified to discuss what should be taught and learned; I leave that to the content experts. But I can and will offer a set of criteria by which to evaluate curricular priorities in order to determine which of them can support a balanced, instructionally helpful assessment system. Regardless of grade level or content area, and for the sake of assessment for student academic well-being, our valued learning targets must be

- Articulated in the form of high-priority achievement standards—clear statements of the essential learnings.
- Reflective of the best current thinking of the content experts in each field of study.
- Arrayed in learning progressions to unfold over time within and across grade levels.
- Unambiguously stated in clear and specific language.
- Prioritized and realistic in number given resources available to teach and learn them.
- Deconstructed into classroom scaffolding that students will climb to master each standard.
- Translated where necessary into student-friendly terms.
- Used to guide learning with consideration of the student's background, interests, and aspirations in deciding what comes next in the learning.
- Competently and confidently mastered by the teachers who are responsible for teaching and assessing them.

Let's analyze each of these criteria in the practical terms a perfect assessment system requires. As we go, we'll consider how these specifications must interact with one another to provide a foundation for productive assessment system and student success.

HIGH-PRIORITY ACHIEVEMENT STANDARDS ARE REQUIRED

Often, the language we use when talking about achievement expectations conveys that we think of them as weapons in the fight for better schools. We see this when political and community leaders contend that the way to increase achievement is to "turn up the heat," "set the bar higher," "make school more challenging," and "instill greater rigor." I already have alluded to the motivational implications of this kind of thinking for students at different places on the achievement continuum. Driving students harder only results in more learning for those who have the confidence that they can succeed. Raising expectations via ever-higher standards spells defeat for those who don't believe they can achieve them. This does not mean we don't need achievement standards; we do. But we need to weave them into the teaching and learning in a different way.

It's also become traditional to define achievement expectations in terms of grade-level achievement by subject. Our standardized testing has reinforced this habit, and over time, society has become convinced that these content segments represent universally agreed-upon domains of achievement that define a student's learning status at a particular point in time. We assume educators all know what it means to say that Mary is at a 3rd grade reading level or that Shawn is doing 6th grade math. But, in fact, very often there is no universal agreement about such expectations—not even across classrooms in the same school building, let alone across buildings, districts, or states. The perfect assessment system seeks agreement on the meaning of academic success across these levels.

As discussed earlier, when we talk about a "domain," we are talking about a large body of content containing a wide range of elements of content knowledge. Whoever is charged with assessing a domain must gather sufficient evidence of student mastery of enough of those wide-ranging elements to support an inference about the extent to which students have mastered all of the content that makes up the domain. This sample needs to be representative in its coverage and sufficient in its depth to infer from each student's score whether that student has mastered the whole domain represented.

In the emerging proficiency-driven (or competence-driven) schools of today, domains are typically defined in the form of long lists of achievement standards. Modern standardized tests are made up of items that align with some of those standards, and taken together, these items are said to "cover" the domain defined by the list. The idea is that one can infer whether a student has mastered the domain's standards based on that student's total score. Qualified experts in the domain examine the sample of items and determine subjectively how many items an examinee must answer correctly to support an inference that the examinee probably has mastered standards that make up the domain. So let's say Shawn attained a score of 30 correct out of 40 items sampling a year's worth of 6th grade math achievement standards. From this, one is to conclude whether Shawn is able to do 6th grade math. The inference-drawing problems are clear. The items did not address all of the standards in the domain—just some of them. Nor is there a sufficient number of items covering any individual standard to support an inference about student mastery of that standard. Because the meaning of Shawn's domain score is unclear in terms of what he actually has achieved, the results provide no basis for deciding what comes next in Shawn's learning. They reveal no path to helpful instructional action.

For the perfect assessment system to become a reality, all thinking about how to document academic success must shift from domain sampling models to a focus on the assessment of each individual high-priority achievement standard. While domain scores have served both accountability and sorting purposes in the past, they lack the informational precision needed to help teachers manage student learning success—an essential aim of the new school mission. And so the perfect system is built to document each student's mastery of each priority standard. To meet accountability needs, evidence of standards mastered can be aggregated over time and across students.

LEARNING TARGETS MUST CAPTURE WHAT'S IMPORTANT

Who gets to decide what is important enough to teach and assess? The most qualified content experts do—those most steeped in the best current thinking of each field of study. Many professional associations have developed achievement standards for their academic discipline (Stiggins & Chappuis, 2017). They include but are not limited to the International Reading Association, the National Council of Teachers of English, the National Council of Teachers of Mathematics, the National Academy of Sciences, the American Association for the Advancement of Science, the National Science Teachers Association, the National Council for the Social Studies, the Center for Civic Education, the Geography Education National Implementation Project, the International Society for Technology in Education, the National Association for Sport and Physical Education, the American Alliance for Theatre and Education, the Arts Education Partnership, the State Education Agency Directors of Arts Education, the National Association for Music Education, and the American Council on the Teaching of Foreign Languages. Local or state teams can tap these organizations' standards or locate others online.

As an assessment specialist and curriculum outsider, I have witnessed two frustrating difficulties related to the content side of testing. The first is that content specialists often struggle to agree on priority standards, and the other is that they seem unable to limit the number of standards to be taught, learned, and assessed to what is reasonable given available instructional resources.

All of us have witnessed national debates and intense local arguments about what it means to be a proficient reader, writer, student of science, and so on. As someone who offers assessment advice to people in instructional leadership positions, I often tell clients that it's possible to assess virtually any learning target they can identify and clearly define. If disagreement emerges on the definitions or priorities among standards, I advise them to just choose the targets that everyone agrees are important, leave any controversial ones aside for now, and proceed. If there are two competing schools of thought about meaning or priorities, I suggest aligning themselves with one side or the other simply so that everyone can move forward toward instruction, learning, and assessment. *There are classrooms full of students awaiting your leadership,* I tell them. *Just decide.*

The perfect assessment system eases this challenge and accommodates differences of opinion by allowing standards definition and prioritization to play out at three levels: state, district, and school/classroom.

At the state level, departments of education can collaborate with local districts' curriculum leaders to select a *very* limited number of the very highest-priority standards for accountability purposes—just a few, really big deal, critically important learnings that all participants can agree on and endorse. It is not a good idea, or even feasible, for this list to include or somehow sample everything anyone could feel is valuable in reading, writing, science, math, and so on. It should be limited to just the top essentials, and the reason for this is simple, commonsense practicality: When it comes to assessment for public accountability, communities just want enough evidence to be confident that their schools are delivering on the essentials that all agree define school success. Once endorsed by all stakeholders, these standards become the central core for teaching, learning, and accountability statewide. But they are not the only valued targets to be learned and assessed.

Districts and their communities may feel strongly that a few additional high-priority achievement standards must be added to the state's list to address local learning priorities in their schools. In the perfect system I envision, they have the option of doing so, and for taking local responsibility for assessment and reporting to the community.

Still further, individual schools and teachers also may want to supplement state and local district lists with achievement expectations they feel are sufficiently important to be included in the evaluation of their school or classroom work. Such opportunities for addition can give voice to important subgroups within the community. In these cases, assessment of student mastery of these targets becomes a local or classroom responsibility.

By now, some of you may be questioning the wisdom of this layered approach to establishing achievement expectations, wary of the multilevel assessment challenges it presents. Fear not! Those challenges are easily met if we are willing to think outside of the traditional testing box (or discard the box altogether). The relief comes from the wide range of potential sources of evidence that can be brought to bear, combined with reliance on modern information management technologies. I'll provide specific details about this in Chapter 6.

Or perhaps your doubts go back to the fundamental question of whether it's even possible for content experts to agree on this short list of highest-priority standards that define academic success. I understand this concern, which lies at the heart of many of the indictments of our long-standing standardized testing tradition. If, in fact, we really do not agree on what it means to succeed in school, what is it that we've been testing in the service of accountability over the past 70 years? These testing traditions have perpetuated the belief that there is something called a 3rd grade reading level, that everyone agrees on what that means, and that all accountability tests can tell us who has reached it and who has not. Further, we have been led to believe that those universally agreed-upon content priorities have been tested consistently over the years with tests that are sufficiently sensitive to detect and permit the evaluation of changes in instructional effectiveness. But if this is not the case, due to deep disagreements on the meaning of academic success and the instructional insensitivity of the tests (Popham & Ryan, 2012), serious questions arise about our assessment legacy. The perfect assessment system puts these uncertainties to rest by redefining academic success in pedagogically defensible terms. Read on to learn how.

LEARNING PROGRESSIONS ARE REQUIRED

If the emerging collections of achievement standards are to contribute to continuous student growth, they must be organized in learning progressions (Heritage, 2010). These successions of standards must be arrayed to unfold over time within and across grade levels or across sequences of courses in the same discipline. Only then can teachers rely on an assessment of a student's current status as a way to understand—and as a way to help the student understand—what should come next in his or her learning. In a perfect assessment system, student growth is described in terms of the student's newly attained place on each relevant learning progression. Instructionally, this is far more helpful than an ill-defined change in a domain-sampling standardized test score.

Progressions cast achievement expectations in terms of prerequisites for the learning that will follow. For example, if students are to master science knowledge, how will that content unfold for them as they advance from grade to grade? How will math reasoning progress from the basics of algebra through calculus? Many of the collections of standards published by the professional associations identified on page 51 are articulated in these terms. Locally developed progressions of achievement standards will work best when conceived in this manner.

Here's a place where I must go beyond my professional expertise in making an assertion regarding academic standards: Each standard in a learning progression should capture what qualified experts in the field regard as truly important learning that provides a key link in the ascending expectations. Those who study and promote our thinking about learning progressions refer to finding the optimal "grain size," which means each piece of it—each foundational subskill or bit of enabling knowledge teachers must teach and students must master—must be neither too sweeping nor too narrow. For lack of a better guideline, and given the limited resources that permeate education, I will simply advocate for relatively few learning targets—rarely more than 10 per subject at the elementary school level and in any middle or high school course. Although the learning targets would be modest in number, each would be broad enough in scope to encapsulate a truly important piece of learning.

Also, curriculum experts often contend that learning does not always unfold in a predictable linear manner. It may come in chunks and leaps rather than incremental steps, depending on the context. Some such patterns of learning or thinking arise from the traditions of certain cultures (Guild, 1994). Such spontaneous jumps sideways or forward can be accommodated in curricular and assessment planning as long as someone familiar with the context within which they might arise can anticipate their potential form and nature in an intellectually and pedagogically appropriate form. This kind of accommodation maximizes the quality assessment of student mastery of any and every learning target. Readers interested in learning more about learning progressions will find helpful information in Heritage (2013).

LEARNING TARGETS MUST BE UNAMBIGUOUSLY STATED

Within a perfect assessment system, each achievement standard is clearly and completely stated in language that trained educators can agree carries the same meaning. The test of agreement is that two or more qualified interpreters of the meaning of a standard, working independently, can restate that standard in their own words and agree on what it means. Qualified interpreters are those who have received training in the academic discipline in question and have established a strong knowledge base. Unambiguously stated standards, as opposed to ones that are essentially Rorschach inkblots, provide a solid basis for assessment and instruction.

We must remember that, with the help of their teachers, students can hit any learning target that they can see and understand and that "holds still" for them. So their success hinges on the clarity of the thinking and language of the adults who are guiding their learning. If there is disagreement among the faculty on the meaning of a particular standard, once again, they need to either abandon that standard or find a compromise meaning. Just decide and move forward on that basis.

LEARNING TARGETS MUST BE REALISTIC IN NUMBER GIVEN RESOURCES

Another almost universal problem to which I have already referred occurs when teams of content experts work to assemble collections of achievement standards and simply cannot limit them to a manageable number in light of the resources available for schools to teach and assess them. When defining what it means to be competent in their particular academic discipline, those who have spent their careers analyzing and expanding their expertise see differentiations and nuances that capture the true complexity of their domain. Their scholarship is most often impeccable... and overwhelming to those not so deeply invested.

In schools and classrooms, practical reality must find a way to step in. As a general rule, districts, schools, and teachers are presented with too many standards given classroom time and assessment resources. When faced with long lists of standards and insufficient resources, assessors will always point out that assessment of each and every standard is impractical. Their solution, as we have established, has been to define the unmanageably long list of standards as "domains" and build tests that sample the domains, not the individual standards within. So the problem gets solved in a way that is more practical in assessment terms than in instructional terms.

The solution is a perfect assessment system that serves both agents of accountability *and* student/teacher teams by calling for a prioritized and limited number of standards. That job falls to those most qualified by content expertise and leadership responsibility.

STANDARDS MUST BE HIGH, BUT LADDERS MUST BE PROVIDED

Remember from our earlier discussion of assessment purposes that the perfect assessment system sets its highest priority as *promoting* student success and not merely measuring it. This dovetails with the rationale for requiring learning progressions, which is that we must provide ways for students and their teachers to see a clear pathway to ongoing learning success.

But we must remember that mastery is not guaranteed or instantaneous. It's what happens day to day in the classroom—over time and with practice—that determines how well and how quickly students travel along the learning progression and ascend the scaffolding that leads them to master a standard.

For example, to begin with, students might master the foundational knowledge needed to be successful with a particular standard. But depending on the learning target they are pursuing, they may also need to become proficient with certain patterns of reasoning—ways of using that knowledge in a problem-solving way. Their teacher must recognize this and provide the appropriate instruction and practice. Another learning target might require mastery of performance skills or product-development capabilities that contribute to ultimate success. These, too, must be identified, taught, and monitored as students grow.

The point is, instructional and assessment planning require that each high-priority standard be deconstructed into its appropriate scaffolding so that teachers and students can rely on ongoing classroom assessment to accurately chart progress toward success. Students need to see the targets in student-friendly terms at the outset of instruction. As they are learning, ongoing self-assessment can help them see and understand the evidence that they are climbing the ladder toward mastery and are closer to their goal today than they were yesterday. This is what will keep students striving and feeling in control of their own chances of success. I will delve into this motivational principle in Chapter 8.

LEARNING TARGETS MUST BE TRANSLATED INTO STUDENT-FRIENDLY TERMS

The perfect assessment system operates in a completely open and honest academic environment—one where there are no surprises and no excuses. That means the learning targets will be made public for all to see and understand in advance of instruction and accountability. It's especially important that students see and understand them. I mentioned this just a moment ago, but it's important enough to repeat in its own section.

Academic expectations can and should be shown to students both in language they can understand and with actual examples of the achievement outcomes they should aspire to reach. It is only with this kind of clarity that students can track their progress over time up the scaffolding toward success. If they know where they're headed and where they are now in relation to that aspiration, then they can partner with their teacher to select strategies that keep them on winning streaks.

LEARNING TARGETS SHOULD CONSIDER STUDENT BACKGROUND, INTERESTS, AND ASPIRATIONS

We create schools that lead students through prescribed learning progressions because we believe there are foundations of academic success that will set students up for lifelong learning success. Much of what I am advocating herein rests on the belief that we can agree once and for all on what the most important of those foundations are. Assessment for accountability and for all other purposes demands that we find that agreement.

However, as our students ascend through the grade levels, the learning targets we set for them must align with their emerging aspirations. Given the pace of our culture's evolution and diversification, we have no idea what today's children may be doing in 20 or 30 years. The energy they devote to their learning while in school increases in proportion to their interest in what they are learning. By promoting their curiosity, we increase the chances of their success and help them build the confidence they need to risk striving for more learning success. So, to the extent that we welcome students into the decision-making process of selecting at least some of their own learning targets as they mature, we encourage them to pursue their own independent pathways to learning.

This kind of student involvement can allow those of diverse cultures in the same school to develop their own culturally sustaining learning foci. It can also inform modifications of achievement expectations for students with special needs as well as accommodations to slow or speed up the pace of learning. These and other such adjustments allow student/teacher teams to select learning pathways that make it possible for all students to find success.

By factoring student voice into decisions about what kind of learning they pursue as they ascend to ever-higher levels of academic attainment, we afford all students equal opportunities to grow in what they believe are productive ways for them. From that point, ongoing self-assessment of their own success generates evidence they need for self-correction. If we don't define lifelong learner in these terms, I don't know how else to define it.

LEARNING TARGETS MUST BE MASTERED BY THE TEACHERS WHO TEACH AND ASSESS THEM

If our goal is merely to produce a dependable rank order of students based on achievement at high school graduation, then the content expertise and assessment literacy of teachers sort of doesn't matter. As students progress through the grade levels, and as their teachers assess their achievement, those teachers may create and use low-quality assessments that yield undependable results. Some will overestimate students' true achievement, while others will underestimate it. Over 13 years, these "errors of measurement" will cancel each other out, and averages will provide a basis for a relatively dependable rank order of students. Mission accomplished, if only in a very inelegant and imprecise manner.

But, as we know, the mission of schools has expanded. Now that teachers also are expected to deliver mastery of pre-set lifelong learner achievement standards, it's a real problem if the teachers involved lack content expertise and create low-quality assessments that yield inaccurate or at least misleading evidence. The result will be inept classroom assessment and unproductive instructional decisions that will impede learning progress. Unless teachers know their assigned content progressions backward and forward, they will have great difficulty diagnosing needs and making productive decisions in the classroom—and so will their students.

And so, for this reason, in this age of "every student ready for college or workplace training," every teacher absolutely must be a competent, confident master of the achievement standards that are his or her assigned responsibility. Only then can they develop or select and use high-quality assessments in beneficial ways.

A NOTE ON AFFECTIVE TARGETS

Our hopes and aspirations for our students have always extended beyond mere academic achievement. We double down on those hopes when we ask our schools to help every student become a lifelong learner. All students need to come to value learning, invest in their own success, learn how to control and take responsibility for their learning, pursue their own interests, develop and maintain strong positive attitudes, and believe that success is within reach for them. I mention this not because teachers can or necessarily should measure these kinds of affective characteristics (although these characteristics certainly are measurable), but because affective characteristics represent dimensions we can help our students develop.

We can use the classroom assessment process to help in this endeavor in one very specific way, and that's by helping our students succeed at learning— by getting them on winning streaks and showing them how to keep winning. Success in the classroom is the foundation of the development of the positive affect that defines a lifelong learner. The human brain is wired to like succeeding, and success triggers the confidence needed to risk the effort required to attain more learning success. I will address specific strategies related to this goal in Chapter 8's look at assessment and student motivation. But for now, suffice it to say that academic success and student affect are inexorably intertwined, and that a perfect assessment system can tap into and help students develop a desire to succeed, confidence in their ability to succeed, motivation to strive, a sense of the value of their relationship with their teacher, and a sense of control over their own academic well-being.

Readers interested in the measurement of these kinds of affective student characteristics can find guidance in Anderson and Bourke (2000). Because values, attitudes, interests, aspirations, and sense of academic efficacy vary in direction (positive to negative) and in intensity (strong to weak), questionnaires with rating scales are a good way to gather evidence of the current state of student affect.

SOUND ASSESSMENT REQUIRES QUALITY LEARNING TARGETS

In summary, the watchword regarding achievement expectations in the perfect assessment system is *precision*. We will rely on qualified experts to articulate high-priority, clear, and specific achievement standards in learning progressions that unfold over time within and across grade levels. These are the learning targets that will be assessed in all contexts. Those that we agreed are high-priority learning targets across the districts in the state will be the limited focus of state accountability assessment. Local education agencies will be free to add their own priority standards to the curricular list from the state, as will individual schools and teachers. In this way, differences of opinion about priorities will be accommodated. Priority standards will be deconstructed into scaffolding that leads students to mastery and will be translated, as needed, into student-friendly terms. And all teachers will be competent masters of the standards they are to help their students master.

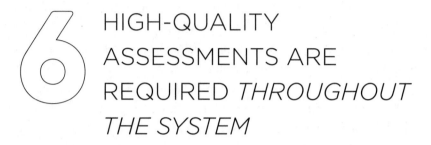

HIGH-QUALITY ASSESSMENTS ARE REQUIRED *THROUGHOUT THE SYSTEM*

Accuracy of observation is the equivalent of accuracy of thinking.

—WALLACE STEVENS

We all remember being assessed during our years in school. As it turns out, those memories can actually function as barriers to quality assessment practice in our schools and classrooms today. The school environments most of us were raised in left us with a dispositional bias: the perspective that being evaluated is a potentially dangerous enterprise, that tests mean the possibility of failure, and that test failure is something we must strive to avoid. Many of us were happy to get out of school and put those feelings behind us…with the exception of that recurring dream in which the final exam is tomorrow and we haven't studied for it!

This generalized assessment anxiety is compounded by the measurement community, in both universities and the testing industry, which has been complicit in practitioners' tendency to keep assessment at arm's length. It does this by defining and discussing assessment in off-putting, complex psychometric ideas and terminology that few outside the measurement community can or want to understand.

And so a stark divide has grown between those who teach and those who assess, and the result is far too many practitioners who lack the assessment literacy needed to do their jobs. It's not just that we are generally uncomfortable with assessment but also that we often choose to remain unschooled in the differences between sound and unsound assessments and, thus, are unable to assure assessment quality in our particular context, whether that's the local district level, the school level, or within our own classrooms.

This chapter attempts to counter that disposition by defining practical standards of test quality in commonsense terms that we can talk about in everyday language. Whether creating or selecting assessments for use, in a perfect assessment system, all professional educators will understand, embrace, and master those standards of quality. I believe that once all stakeholders understand what truly sound assessment practices look like, those practices will become something to embrace and invest in rather than fear.

THE STANDARDS OF ASSESSMENT QUALITY

So far, we have established that one starting place for the creation of a quality assessment in any context is a clear articulation of the purpose it is to serve. When we begin with a clear sense of the intended user's information needs, we can build the assessment to meet those needs. The other starting place is well-articulated learning targets that can be precisely and accurately represented in both test exercises and scoring schemes.

Once we have a clear and complete picture of the assessment context in these terms, we are ready to begin developing or selecting an assessment. There are four critical assessment design guidelines to follow. Each new assessment or previously developed assessment of choice must

1. Rely on a *proper assessment method* given the learning target to be assessed.

2. *Sample enough evidence* to lead to a dependable inference about the level of student attainment.

3. Be built of *high-quality ingredients* (test items or exercises and scoring procedures).

4. Anticipate and minimize the effects of any *sources of bias* that can distort results.

These are universally accepted and non-negotiable standards of excellence in assessment that apply in every assessment context. Fail on any of these four fronts, and the assessment probably will yield undependable results that will misrepresent the current state of the examinee's learning.

If we are to meet these standards of excellence in assessment, we must establish a universal foundation of assessment literacy throughout all of American education. By "universal," I mean that everyone or anyone forming or expressing a judgment regarding matters of assessment quality needs to be able to defend their evaluative statements with at least a fundamental understanding of principles of sound assessment. I'm talking about practitioners, of course, but also policymakers, parents, students themselves, the news media and, through the media, the school community in general. It's instructive to take a closer look at what makes up basic assessment literacy for both professional educators and noneducators. Of course, noneducators don't require as deep an understanding of assessment as professional educators do, and it's instructive to analyze the differences between what represents basic assessment literacy for these two populations. We'll start with the professionals.

ASSESSMENT LITERACY FOR IN-SCHOOL PERSONNEL

An assessment-literate professional educator knows how to gather dependable evidence of student learning using high-quality assessments and how to use the assessment process and its results either to promote student learning or to certify it, depending on the context.

The Matter of Proper Assessment Method

A truly sound assessment of student learning relies on an assessment method capable of dependably reflecting the learning target in question. As it turns out, we need to assess just a few kinds of achievement, and we have just a few assessment methods at our disposal. If only we had an algorithm for matching the two, meeting this standard of quality would be easy, right? Well, we do, and it is. It's just that too few practitioners know of it.

The easy-to-use algorithm, framed in Figure 2, holds that any specific learning target identified as important for students to master will fall into one of four categories: (1) mastery of *content knowledge*, (2) mastery of the ability to use that knowledge to *reason and solve some sort of problem*, (3) development of demonstrable physical *performance skills*, and (4) development of the ability to create achievement-related *products* that meet standards of quality.

Further, the array of assessment methods available to reflect these four categories of mastery is similarly limited. Here are the four choices; there are no others: (1) *selected-response* methods (multiple choice, true/false, matching), (2) *written response* methods (short or extended essays), (3) *performance assessment* (based on observation and professional judgment), and (4) *personal communication* (based on direct verbal interaction with the learner).

FIGURE 2
Aligning Assessment Methods to Learning Targets

Learning Target/ Assessment Method	Selected Response	Written Response	Performance Assessment	Personal Communication
Content Knowledge	good match	good match	X	good match
Reasoning and Problem Solving	good match	good match	good match	good match
Performance Skills	X	X	good match	good match for verbal skills
Product Development	X	X	good match	X

Source: CHAPPUIS, JAN; STIGGINS, RICK J.; CHAPPUIS, STEVE; ARTER, JUDITH A., CLASSROOM ASSESSMENT FOR STUDENT LEARNING: DOING IT RIGHT – USING IT WELL, 2nd Ed., ©2012. Adapted by permission of Pearson Education, Inc., New York, New York.

In Figure 2, you can see the various matches between these targets and methods. Some matches make complete sense—they can work. Other cells align methods and targets that make no sense—they cannot work. Any assessor's first challenge is to know the target well enough to pick a method capable of reflecting it. Professional educators must be given the opportunity to become confident, competent masters of properly linking learning targets to assessment methods. In the perfect assessment system, competence in this area is expected and routinely verified.

The Matter of Sound Sampling

Any assessment includes a sample of all of the questions one could ask about the topic if the test could be infinitely long. Obviously, practicality requires that we limit the length of every assessment, so the question that follows is "How much evidence is enough for the assessor to be confident that a student has or has not mastered the learning target?" The answer is a matter of professional judgment. The challenge assessors always face is how to gather enough evidence to support a confident inference about achievement without wasting time gathering too much.

An assessment-literate educator understands that the answer to how much is enough depends on several factors. One is the scope of the learning target—the bigger the scope, the more exercises may be needed to cover it with sufficient depth to support a strong judgment about student proficiency. Another factor is the instructional decision to be made on the basis of the results. The more important the decision (e.g., "Has this student developed the literacy proficiency required for graduation?"), the more certain the assessor needs to be about the soundness of the results, and, therefore, the more exercises should be included. Still another consideration is the amount of testing time available. The more time that's available, the more exercises can be included. In that same vein, the more time it will take for examinees to respond to any one exercise (e.g., multiple choice vs. essay), or the greater the scoring time for responses, the fewer exercises can be included.

Boiling it down, when it comes to sound sampling in any assessment context, we seek maximum quality and efficiency—that is, to gather sufficient information in minimum time, given the assessment's target and purpose. As it turns out, there are specific, well-developed rules of evidence for achieving quality in these terms in any context. My purpose is not to offer that training but to point out that it is readily available (see the Appendix) and to assert that only an assessment-literate educator who is a master of the learning target in question can determine how much evidence is enough in any particular assessment context.

The Matter of Quality Exercises and Scoring Guides

Assessments arrive in schools or classrooms in one of two ways: someone in that context creates it or selects it from a pool of already developed assessments. In either case, to ensure quality, that someone must apply a set of criteria to evaluate the assessment items, exercises, tasks, and scoring schemes. These criteria are not complex or technical. They are relatively easy for any teacher or school leader to master. They have been clearly and completely articulated and illustrated by assessment experts in a variety of sound professional references that you can find listed in the Appendix. So, again, I will not delve into them here.

As mentioned, the array of available assessment methods is limited to four: (1) selected response, (2) written response, (3) performance assessment, and (4) direct verbal interaction with students. All four methods require that the test developer figure out how to use a question or a task to trigger a response from the examinee and how to evaluate that response in light of the intended learning target. In the perfect assessment system, all practitioners have the opportunity to evaluate their own assessment literacy and to develop their professional capacities in this arena if needed. Further, they are accountable for demonstrating those competencies both at the time of their certification and during routine evaluations of their job performance.

The Matter of Bias in Assessment

In any assessment context, factors other than the learner's actual achievement can infiltrate and influence assessment results. When this happens, the results are said to be biased. The direction of a bias can be to either increase or decrease scores. Either kind is unacceptable, as both lead to misrepresentation of the learner's true achievement. For example, if a test item is based on a perspective relevant to members of the dominant culture but not to members of minority subcultures, then that item places members of the dominant culture at an advantage and members of the minority subcultures at a disadvantage. Or bias can enter in the form of characteristics of the assessment itself, as in the case of poorly constructed questions or scoring guides, items written at a reading level that's inappropriately high for the intended examinees, or reliance on poorly trained scorers. Additional problems can arise from characteristics of students themselves, such as extreme test anxiety, illness, or unfamiliarity with the language of the test items. And, finally, an examinee's performance can be influenced by characteristics of the testing environment, such as noise or other distractions, poor lighting, unclear directions, or test administration that relies on technology unfamiliar to examinees.

These represent just a few examples of potential sources of bias that can affect results. The bottom line here is that when factors unrelated to achievement exert influence on test results, the fairness of the assessment is called into question. Assessment-literate educators are prepared to anticipate potential sources of bias and carry out procedures that will minimize distortions. That is, they know what can go wrong and can take steps to address these problems. This is why, as we conceive of a perfect assessment system, we need to be absolutely certain that assessment developers and selectors are able to detect and minimize the effects of sources of bias and distortion.

ASSESSMENT LITERACY FOR LOCAL SCHOOL LEADERS

Clearly, if district and building administrators are to supervise and help develop the assessment literacy of their faculty members, they must be masters of the keys to quality we have been discussing. But their work in this realm does not stop there. They must also lead the process of establishing within their districts the conditions that will permit teachers to transform their knowledge of sound assessment practice into classroom-based action. This will require passage of local policies and regulations that do the following:

- Commit to and develop a balanced assessment system within the district, as defined in Chapter 3.
- Ensure the clear and complete definition of learning targets to be mastered and assessed in all contexts.
- Develop the assessment literacy needed to oversee and assure quality throughout the system.
- Ensure effective communication of assessment results in all contexts.
- Link assessment to positive motivation for all students throughout the system.

Steve Chappuis, Carol Commodore, and I have prepared guidelines and detailed rubrics that enable local leadership teams to (1) conduct comprehensive local district self-evaluations of the extent to which those conditions currently are in place in their schools and classrooms, and (2) take action based on the results of the self-analysis to put them in place (Chappuis, Commodore, & Stiggins, 2017).

ASSESSMENT LITERACY BEYOND SCHOOL

If policymakers at local, state, and federal levels are to set policies and accompanying regulations to guide sound assessment practice, they must bring to that process their *own* understanding of sound assessment practice that is appropriate to the context of today's society and schools. The same is true of parents and members of the school community. In this section, I provide four sample policy realms* that align with the vision of excellence in assessment described so far. The perfect assessment system envisioned herein is guided by community leaders who are prepared to help educators do their assessment jobs.

---

*Note: The ideas covered in this section and the one that follows are adaptations of material first published in the October 2014 edition of *Phi Delta Kappan* (Stiggins, 2014b). They appear here with the permission of the publisher.

The Matter of Assessment and the Mission of Schools

Policymakers, parents, and the school community must understand that "society has changed the mission of its schools. We expect them to do far more than sort students along a continuum of achievement by the end of high school—that is, to do more than merely sort students into the various segments of our social and economic systems. Important new missions have been added, and our assessment practices must accommodate them" (p. 69).

Today we expect our schools to promote much higher levels of achievement than ever before, while narrowing achievement gaps, assuring lifelong learner competencies for all students, promoting universal high school graduation, and making sure all students are ready for college and workplace training. As a result, assessment must do far more than just provide the evidence for grading and ranking students based on their achievement. It must also serve as an instructional tool to help students learn better and more.

The Matter of Assessment Quality

Policymakers, parents, and the school community must understand that "regardless of the purpose, assessments must yield dependable evidence of the level of student attainment of achievement expectations" (p. 69).

Assessment is the process of gathering information to inform instructional decisions, and so it follows that dependable evidence leads to good decisions, and inaccurate evidence (due to inept classroom assessment) leads to counterproductive decisions. Student well-being depends on assessment quality, and there is reason to be concerned about the current quality of the assessments used at all levels of U.S. education. Very few practicing teachers and almost no practicing school leaders have been trained to develop quality assessments or trained to use assessments in effective ways.

The Matter of the Student's Role in Assessment

The inferences students make about themselves based on their interpretation of their own assessment results are as important in determining their school success as the instructional decisions made by their teachers and school leaders based on their interpretation of those results. (p. 70)

Students judge the chances of their future success based on their inter-pretation of the success they have experienced in the past. In their minds, over time, success or failure can take on a life of its own and affect their sense of academic self-efficacy. This is the impetus for the Students' Bill of Assess-ment Rights (see pages 72–73).

The Matter of Evaluating Teacher Performance

Standardized achievement test scores do not provide a measure of school or teacher quality or the means for improving school and teacher quality. They represent "the effect of school factors in combination with other factors beyond the control of teachers and school leaders" (p. 70).

Three points are important here.

First, because of severe limitations in the length and methodology of standardized achievement tests, they reflect only a very narrow band of the learning targets schools and teachers intend for children to master. To find out about student success relative to the rest of those important targets, it's necessary to turn to teachers and the evidence they gather day to day in the classroom.

Second, teachers and schools account for only a small portion of the variability in student performance on such annual tests. The remainder is explained by factors beyond the control of teachers and schools, including

- Aspects of the school, such as class sizes, curriculum materials, instruc-tional time, availability of specialists, and resources for learning (e.g., books, computers, science labs, and more).
- Home and community supports and challenges.
- Individual student needs and abilities, health, and attendance.
- Peer culture and achievement.
- Prior teachers and schooling, as well as other current teachers.
- Differential summer learning loss, which especially affects low-income children.
- The specific test used, which emphasizes some kinds of learning and deemphasizes others and which rarely measures achievement well above or below grade level (Darling-Hammond et al., 2012).

Third, as illustrated in the points just raised, it's time to move beyond this obsessive belief in the universal potency of standardized achievement test scores when it comes to improving school and teacher quality. My point is not that the tests are useless, but that those in policymaking positions must keep them in perspective and balance them with other assessment applications that have proven their worth in the classroom. If scores are not where they should be, the key question is "What can be done within the community and within the school to support student learning?" And this question applies not only to the few learning targets tested annually but also to all of the important learnings schools and teachers offer our children.

STUDENTS' BILL OF ASSESSMENT RIGHTS

Students of all ages and in all educational contexts are vested with certain inalienable rights related to the assessment of their achievement and the use of their assessment results to influence their learning. In Oregon, these rights have been encoded in state law (Oregon Revised Statute 329.479). Students and their families should be made aware of the entitlements, and educators must embrace their professional responsibility to understand and protect them. The perfect assessment system honors all parts of the Students' Bill of Assessment Rights:

1. Students are entitled to understand the purpose for each assessment in which they participate; they have a right to know specifically how the results will be used.

2. Students are entitled to understand the learning target(s) to be reflected in the exercises and scoring guides that make up any and all assessments.

3. Students are entitled to understand the differences between good and poor performance on pending assessments and learn to self-assess in terms of that performance continuum in tracking their progress toward mastery.

4. Students are entitled to dependable assessment of their achievement gathered using quality assessments.

5. Students are entitled to effective communication of their assessment results, whether those results are being delivered to them, to their families, or to others concerned with their academic well-being.

A SUMMARY OF THE KEYS
TO ASSESSMENT QUALITY

As we look to the future, it's clear our assessment system cannot effectively promote and certify student learning unless and until we can count on it to provide dependable evidence of student learning. Historically, we have not been able to count on our assessments in these terms, due to a pervasive lack of opportunities for professional educators or policymakers to develop their assessment literacy. But if there is one thing we know today, it is how to create and effectively use quality assessments. And professional development programs are readily available to teach those lessons to all interested in student learning success.

The most effective of those programs teach practitioners how to meet four non-negotiable standards of quality: (1) how to select a proper assessment method for the context, (2) how to sample student performance in practical terms, (3) how to build or select high-quality exercises and scoring schemes, and (4) how to identify and address potential sources of bias that can distort results.

All that is missing are opportunities for interested educators and members of school communities to learn these principles of sound assessment practice. If we seek perfection, we know where to find it.

EFFECTIVE COMMUNICATION OF ASSESSMENT RESULTS

Self-knowledge is no guarantee of happiness. But it is on the side of happiness and can supply the courage to fight for it.

—SIMONE DE BEAUVOIR

In the very simplest terms, communication is the process of transferring information from a sender to a receiver. When communication is effective, the information arrives in a timely manner, and the receiver understands it well enough to make use of it.

Assessment, in the simplest terms, is the process of gathering information about student achievement to inform educational decisions. When that information has been gathered, the assessor's next task is to communicate it to the intended user who, in turn, uses the information as the basis for decisions intended to enhance learning. So communication about assessment results is effective only when the intended user understands the results and knows how to act on them in the service of promoting learning success.

If we connect the dots, we see why effective communication of assessment results is so important: the quality of the instructional decisions at all levels—classroom, local district, state, and nation—depends upon it. The academic success and well-being of students hangs in the balance. To serve students and their teachers well, assessment results must detail where each student is currently in the relevant progressions of the standards being assessed. Only then can teachers and students decide what should come next in the learning or determine that the student has achieved the appropriate level of attainment. Therefore, effective communication of assessment results requires that two essential conditions be satisfied:

1. **The evidence shared must reflect student achievement accurately and support correct inferences on the part of the intended users.** This requirement can be satisfied only if assessor and user have a common understanding of the nature of the learning target being assessed, and the assessor has ensured the assessment meets all necessary standards of quality.

2. **The information shared must be precise and in terms the users can understand.** This means results are presented at an appropriate level of detail to fit the decision context and are transmitted using words, scores, or illustrations of proficiency that carry the same familiar meaning for the message sender and receiver.

To put it another way, if assessment results cannot support correct inferences about student achievement, if they include content unfamiliar to the recipient, if they are too general or specific for the context, or if they are presented in a language or other format that is foreign to the recipient, then miscommunication is assured. The implications can be profound: discouraged and frustrated decision makers may simply ignore what could and should have been useful information, confusion may cause student and teacher to misinterpret what to do next to promote learning success, discouraged learners hanging on the edge of giving up may be lost, a teacher may overlook a critical "teachable moment," or a teacher may waste valuable time re-teaching that which already has been learned.

OUR HISTORY OF INEFFECTIVE COMMUNICATION

To set the stage for our analysis of the kind of communication of results found in the perfect assessment system, let's think about the two dominant (indeed, iconic) means of communicating student achievement that we have relied on over the decades: grades and test scores. Without question, both have made it easy to manage a great deal of information, and both have served as the basis for a simple behavior management system of reward and punishment suited to schools' historic mission of sorting students according to level of academic attainment.

What grades and test scores have not done, however, and what they *cannot* do, is satisfy our two key requirements for effective communication of assessment results to meet key information needs of students and teachers. Often, they carry no mutually shared meaning for message sender and receiver, making interpretation difficult at best. Further, the information they do convey often is too imprecise to meet the needs of those decision makers who seek to promote learning.

How Report Card Grades Fail Us as Communication

Summary report card grades ease information management challenges in the classroom simply by eliminating most of the information. Even though an individual assignment or assessment in the classroom may reflect student achievement of a number of specific learning targets, when a grade is assigned and entered into the record, all this detail—the areas of strengths and areas for improvement related to these identified learning targets—is hidden behind the overall judgment of quality that the grade represents.

Next, teachers summarize the grades they've assigned to individual tasks and assessments over the course of a grading period by calculating a report card grade, further obscuring the information about students' mastery of specific learning targets reflected across several assessments. Consider that five students who all receive a B on their report card may, in fact, have fundamentally different learning success profiles. A grade-based system of communication simply does not account for this reality. Information that is complex and potentially helpful is lost as it is transformed into something simple and judgmental: A, B, C, D, or F.

Then schools summarize final grades assigned to students over the course of several years to compute a cumulative grade point average for purposes of inter-student comparison, sacrificing information about the differences in the individual student's achievement across the various courses or domains of learning. In this final way, and in order to preserve the appearance of academic rigor that ranking permits, we leave behind all details about student achievement that could otherwise inform us how to promote learning.

How Test Scores Miss the Mark

Test scores, as historically conceived and used in U.S. education, hide the valuable details of student learning just as grades do. Any helpful specifics they might have provided regarding student strengths or areas for improvement— again, specifics that could inform decisions that would boost student learning —are sacrificed in the service of information management efficiency.

College admissions tests represent a case in point. Their mission has been to reveal differences in levels of achievement. The same is true of accountability-focused standardized tests administered at individual grades. Standard scores, percentile ranks, and grade equivalent scores that sample broad achievement domains arrive once a year (often after students have already moved on to the next grade level and teacher) and offer little by way of instructional insight, whether referenced at school, local district, state, national, or interplanetary levels. Given the historic institutional mission of schools, all of this makes complete communication sense. As noted in Chapter 2, though, the redesigned SAT, which provides diagnostic information on student needs for instructional planning, is an encouraging indicator that the tide is beginning to turn toward better communication of results.

A NEW SCHOOL MISSION BRINGS NEW DEMANDS FOR BETTER COMMUNICATION

In addition to ranking students based on achievement, schools are now also charged with narrowing the achievement gap and attaining universal high school graduation. This means they are to evaluate students, teachers, school leaders, and schools in terms of how achievement improves year to year.

To do that we need the details about students' mastery of specific learning targets—the very same details universally sacrificed under the old regime. We need new and better ways to manage and communicate this previously discarded, instructionally relevant information while at the same time permitting summaries of achievement for those who need information at that level to inform their decisions. The perfect system defined herein can serve all users. It does this by starting with clearly defined maps of pathways to academic achievement within disciplines and transforming the learning targets in those maps into quality assessments, the results of which are fed into modern information management technologies capable of reporting results in that form of specific learning targets mastered for individual students and summaries over student groups.

At the classroom level, we need every teacher in every classroom to

- Have instructional responsibility for helping his or her students master a clear and appropriate set of important achievement standards that fit into long-term progressions for academic success.
- Be a confident and competent master of all the learning targets he or she is charged with teaching.
- Dependably assess student mastery of those targets, whether during learning for formative purposes or to certify attainment in summative contexts.
- Maintain dependable records of each student's place in each relevant learning progression and be able to pass these on to next year's teacher at the end of the school year.
- Be free to accommodate differences in the rates of students' learning.
- Know when and how to employ principles of assessment FOR learning so as to engage students in ongoing self-assessment experiences that maximize their motivation, engagement, and learning success.

The constellation of assessment and instructional realities listed here form the foundation of a totally new, effective, and efficient means of communicating of assessment results—one that preserves all of the useful information that assessments can provide and meets all the needs of instructional decision makers.

EFFECTIVE COMMUNICATION AS A FUNCTION OF ASSESSMENT PURPOSE

Let's return to Figure 1 on pages 43–44 in Chapter 4 for a reminder of the purposes assessment can serve within a perfect system:

- Teachers use *classroom assessment* formatively to help them discover and address student needs and to inform students of strengths and areas in need of improvement in an assessment FOR learning context. And, of course, teachers also use assessment for summative purposes, measuring and reporting the sufficiency of student learning at the end of a grading period.
- At the school and district levels, teams of teachers and school leaders use *periodic interim/benchmark assessments*—common assessments across classrooms or schools that yield comparable results—to discover common themes of student needs or to map necessary changes in instructional priorities over time.
- Teachers, curriculum leaders, and school leaders use the results of *annual tests* to inform longer-term program effectiveness and school improvement decisions that affect program adoptions and patterns of resource allocation.

Neither summary grades nor test scores purporting to represent entire achievement domains can communicate assessment results in sufficient detail to meet the demands of the formative and summative applications outlined in Figure 1—not at any level.

In the classroom context, grades and test scores do not convey the diagnostic information that can help teachers pinpoint and address student strengths or weaknesses, nor do they provide teachers with anything substantive to pass on to students in order to enhance their understanding of how to achieve success or help them engage in self-assessment. So in formative and assessment FOR learning situations, there is no role for grades and numerical test scores. Rather, students need continuous access to descriptive feedback that describes their work and informs them about how to do better next time.

Given this feedback, they will be able to track and understand changes in their own academic capabilities over time.

Moving to summative applications, the classroom teacher's challenge is to make a summary judgment about the sufficiency of student achievement given the particular learning targets. Our report card grading traditions dictate that this be done by combining test scores into an academic average to be mapped on a pre-set letter-grade scale. Consider this more effective communication strategy: Start instruction on day one by sharing with students a list of the priority achievement standards to be taught, learned, and assessed during the grading period. As instruction unfolds, conduct an assessment for each of those standards as it comes up during the grading period. Base each student's end-of-course grade on the proportion of standards mastered. Accompany the grade with a list of the course achievement standards the student has and has not mastered. This would actually be informative—useful both to the student and his or her family and to the next year's teacher.

Let's change context. Let's assume a professional learning community (PLC) has created and administered a common interim/benchmark assessment for use across classrooms to provide a test score that reflects student mastery of a domain of standards. If the PLC members are looking for the kind of precise data they need to identify strengths and weaknesses across students or classrooms, this approach will not provide it. But what if they created assessments built to provide evidence for dependable inferences about individual student mastery of individual learning targets? Then faculty teams could use the results to identify facets of their instruction in need of improvement.

It is common practice these days for schools and districts to form "data teams" to pore over annual standardized tests for insights on where they might be able to improve instruction. To the extent that test publishers provide score reports that subdivide achievement domains into their individual achievement standards, include enough items in the tests to support inferences on the extent of student mastery of each standard, and report results accordingly, the careful analysis of those results by data team members certainly can be formatively useful. The smart decision at the local level is to screen standardized tests to find those that assess and report in this manner. However, the perfect system I envision accomplishes this in a far more efficient manner.

TRULY EFFECTIVE COMMUNICATION AT WORK IN THE CLASSROOM

Years ago, my colleague Anne Davies shared the story of one middle school teacher's experience with truly effective communication of achievement results. Now, I share it in almost every workshop I do with teachers.

This teacher (we'll call her Ms. Murphy) had committed to engaging her students as partners in telling the story of their own growth by replacing traditional parent-teacher conferences with student-led conferences. She had prepared her students for success very carefully by

- Basing her instruction on very clear learning targets, which she shared with students from the outset of instruction.
- Developing high-quality assessments of those targets.
- Engaging students in ongoing self-assessment as they learned.
- Having each student build a growth portfolio full of examples of his or her work as it changed over time to present to and discuss with parents.
- Giving students class time to practice their conference presentations with one another, which not only helped them improve their presentation skills but also prompted them to reflect further on their learning gains.

The student-led conferences were scheduled for the late afternoon and staggered so that there were three or four families meeting in the classroom at a time. Students welcomed their family members as they arrived, introduced them to Ms. Murphy, retrieved their portfolios from the file, and ushered their family to a designated table, where they gave their presentations, shared their work and its results, and discussed their progress with their families. Ms. Murphy circulated among the tables, contributing as needed.

As she walked by one table, she was surprised to hear a student conducting his conference in Spanish. He had not practiced this way, but all involved—his mom, dad, grandmother, and younger sibling—were paying rapt attention. Although Ms. Murphy didn't speak Spanish herself, she could see that this student was proceeding through his growth portfolio, sharing the learning targets and describing his successes and challenges with actual examples of his work. At the end of his presentation, his family applauded.

As they were leaving, Ms. Murphy met them at the door and thanked them for coming. Last to leave was Grandma, who simply clasped Ms. Murphy's hand with tears in her eyes and said "thank you" in English. When they were gone, Ms. Murphy commented to her student on his use of Spanish and asked him how the conference had gone. The student replied that when his family talks about really important things and Grandma is there, they do so in Spanish, to include and honor her. The family meeting had gone very well, he said. Ms. Murphy could see that it had. She could see how proud his family was and that he felt immensely successful.

This, I submit, is truly effective communication of assessment results. Everyone involved understood the meaning of academic success. It was OK for students not to be good at particular tasks at the beginning of instruction because they were just getting started. Ms. Murphy helped them understand the learning targets they needed to hit. All involved were partners in the accumulation of evidence showing changes in student performance over time. Students came to their conferences with both an understanding of the targets and the vocabulary needed to talk about them with their families. But the real pride for the students came from knowing they had grown and being able to prove it to all who asked. They felt their own strength and confidence.

A SUMMARY OF PERFECT COMMUNICATION

In our perfect assessment system, effective communication about assessment results means that the information we share helps users make sound decisions that improve learning. The conditions necessary to achieve this arise from successful completion of the work outlined in Chapter 5's look at learning targets and Chapter 6's look at high-quality assessment.

Only if learning targets are clearly, completely, and appropriately defined in learning progressions that unfold over time within and across grade levels is it possible for teachers, students, and other stakeholders to understand the meaning of academic success and work to achieve it. Further, in all assessment contexts, the information gathered and results generated must lead to sound inferences about student mastery of each relevant learning target. When both these conditions are satisfied, we have the foundation in place for effective communication that offers all students the greatest chance to ascend their relevant learning progressions. As they do, all interested parties—including the learners themselves—can stay abreast of this success.

USING ASSESSMENT TO MOTIVATE *ALL* STUDENTS

Correction does much, but encouragement does more.

—JOHANN WOLFGANG VON GOETHE

We in the measurement community have been inappropriately narrow in our thinking by seeing excellence in assessment only in terms of reliability, validity, and fairness. Overlooked in this list is the critical importance of the emotional—and, therefore, *educational*—impact of the assessment process on the learner. You might show me the most valid and reliable assessment in the world, but if the results it generates lead students to give up in hopelessness, it may not be a high-quality assessment, for the simple reason that it may do far more harm than good. In other words, matters of assessment quality cannot be addressed in a comprehensive manner without thoughtful consideration of the context within and manner in which an assessment is used and the impact it actually has on student learning.

Many in the measurement community may well recoil at this assertion, contending that the only things assessment technicians can control are the characteristics of the assessment itself and the validity and reliability of its results. Conditions of assessment use are under the control of teachers, school officials, and policymakers. If they use the test to serve a purpose for which it is not validated, those local users need to take responsibility for its impact. If they administer it in ways that introduce distortions in the scores, the test developer is not responsible. If, for example, the social context within which it is used ends up harming learners, then local users are culpable.

But if we in the measurement community understand how to promote productive use of assessments from the classroom to the boardroom—or if we understand the keys to the most effective use of tests in important contexts to prevent harm to students—which we do—then it is our responsibility to help local users become sufficiently assessment literate to conduct and use assessments in the most productive ways. It's this spirit that informs this chapter's discussion.

The perfect assessment system promotes effective use in very specific ways. To illustrate how, I must address a topic that has been long neglected in the development of U.S. assessment systems: our understanding of and ability to integrate into practice the emotional dynamics of the assessment experience from the student's point of view.

THE EMOTIONAL DYNAMICS OF STUDENT LEARNING SUCCESS

As we build the perfect assessment system, we can rely on one of the most important educational breakthroughs of the 21st century to provide the new emotional dynamics we will need: the idea of using "assessment FOR learning." I've talked about this a bit in earlier chapters, but I'd like to go into specific, strategic detail about its inner workings. This idea was first labeled by Black (1986), and it has now been under development for three decades by an international team of us striving to enhance the instructional power of assessment.

The key "assessment FOR learning" insight that has emerged for us is as follows: *A student's emotional response to assessment results will determine what that student decides to do about those results: keep working, or give up.* In this context, it's essential to understand that anxiety and vulnerability are enemies of learning. When one tries to learn and fails, the experience can trigger uncertainty about one's ability to learn. The resulting loss of "smart status" and fear of future failure can freeze cognition; if this becomes chronic, it can give rise to hopelessness and pessimism in the classroom. When a student is on a losing streak—has fallen into a pattern of what he or she believes to be inevitable failure—it's easy to lose heart and see no option but to give up. If that student is unlucky, a naïve adult or two will decide that if a little intimidation doesn't motivate success in school, a great deal of intimidation just might. This is exactly the wrong approach.

In Figure 3, you'll see a brief analysis of the differences in the assessment experience of students who are succeeding and students who are failing. Please study these differences before reading on.

Given our new school mission built around raising the level of all students' success, narrowing achievement gaps, and preparing all students for college or workplace training, I submit we need assessment strategies that shift as many students as possible from the losing streak side of Figure 3's continuum to the winning streak side. Quite simply, students on the verge of hopelessness need hope. Those who keep losing need a win. Assessment's role in a classroom that embraces assessment FOR learning is to deliver ongoing learning success, turn one win into a winning streak, and promote optimism and confidence.

So how do we get started? My colleague Jan Chappuis (2015) instructs us on these matters in the second edition of her book *Seven Strategies of Assessment FOR Learning*. Her strategies focus on ensuring students always know and understand the answers to three key questions:

- "Where am I going?" (i.e., "What am I trying to learn?")
- "Where am I now in relation to those learning expectations?"
- "How can I close the gap between where I am now and where I want to be?"

Students continually in touch with answers to these questions are in a position to watch themselves grow over time or take corrective action if they are not improving, and either way, this helps them maintain a strong internal sense of control over their chances of success. They are active, empowered participants in their own learning.

Jan explains that to help students see and understand where they're headed, teachers should begin instruction by sharing student-friendly versions of the learning targets. Then they should share examples of student work that illustrate the performance continuum they will be traveling, from

FIGURE 3

Contrasting Dynamics of the Assessment Experiences

Students on Winning Streaks	Students on Losing Streaks
What assessment results provide:	
Continuous evidence of success	Continuous evidence of failure
Likely effect on the learner:	
Hope rules; remains optimistic	Hopelessness dominates
Success fuels productive action	Initial panic gives way to resignation
What the student is probably thinking in the face of results:	
"It's all good; I'm doing fine"	"This hurts; I'm not safe here"
"See the trend? I succeed as usual"	"I can't do *this* either"
"I want more success"	"I'm confused; I don't like this–help!"
"We focus on what I do well"	"Why is it always about what I can't do?"
"I know what to do next"	"Nothing I do ever seems to work "
"Move on, grow, learn new stuff"	"Defend, hide, get away from here"
"Feedback helps me"	"Feedback hurts me–scares me"
"Public success feels very good"	"Public failure is embarrassing"
"I can make the difficult make sense"	"I can't make this make sense"
Actions likely to be taken by the learner:	
Take risks–stretch, go for it!	Trying is too dangerous–retreat, escape
Seek what is new and exciting	Avoid new stuff
Seek challenges	Seek what's easy
Practice with gusto	Don't practice
Take initiative	Avoid initiative
Persist	Give up
Likely result of these actions:	
Lay foundations now for success later	Can't master prerequisites needed later
Success becomes THE reward	No success–no reward
Self-enhancement	Self-defeat, self-destruction
Positive self-fulfilling prophecy	Negative self-fulfilling prophecy
Extending the effort in face of difficulty	Giving up quickly in face of difficulty
Acceptance of responsibility	Denial of responsibility
Making success public	Covering up failure (cheating)
Self-analysis applied to win	Self-criticism is the easy default
Manageable stress	Stress remains high
Curiosity, enthusiasm	Boredom, frustration, fear
Resilience	Yielding quickly to defeat
Continuous adaptation	Inability to adapt

Source: From *Revolutionize Assessment: Empower Students, Inspire Learning* (pp. 46–47), by R. J. Stiggins, 2014, Thousand Oaks, CA: Corwin. Copyright 2014 by Corwin. Adapted with permission.

poor-quality work to mid-range work to high-quality work. Keeping these examples readily available for consultation and comparison allows students to chart their own work's evolution toward quality and watch themselves ascend the scaffolding to success.

To help students see *where they are now in relation to ultimate success* as they are learning and growing, Jan recommends replacing periodic judgmental feedback on student work (i.e., grades) with the practice of giving students continuous access to descriptive feedback on their work. This is feedback that describes key attributes of the work in ways that inform the student how to do better the next time. Then, as the learning proceeds, teachers must focus on elevating the students' (a) understanding of the learning target and its vocabulary, (b) grasp of the performance continuum—that is, why poor work is poor and good work is good, and (c) ability to transform the descriptive feedback they've received into self-assessment skills that will permit them to begin generating their own descriptive feedback and partner with their teacher in determining how to do better the next time. Notice how the locus of control shifts over time from the teacher to the student? It does so in immensely productive ways that I will discuss shortly.

Finally, to help students understand how to *narrow the gap between where they are now in relation to where they want to be,* Jan recommends teachers deliver lessons focused on improving the quality of work one key attribute at a time. This includes giving students time to engage in focused revision of their work as they come to understand the attributes of quality, and prompting continuous reflection on changes they see in the quality of their work. She even suggests providing students with opportunities to communicate with one another and with their families about those changes, with the proviso that they be able to back up their assertions with evidence found in actual samples of their work.

The practical key to assessment FOR learning is that, over time, responsibility for formative assessment shifts from the teacher to the individual student. If the foundation for this transition is properly laid, students will embrace this new responsibility with great enthusiasm, and learning will skyrocket. We have decades of compelling evidence, gathered around the world, documenting profound achievement gains for all learners (half to three-quarters of a standard deviation or more), with large gains accruing for learners with a history of struggling in school (Black & Wiliam, 1998a, 1998b; Hattie & Timperley, 2007). Inexpensive and very effective professional development is readily available for teachers and school leaders who wish to tap this fountain of learning success (see the Appendix).

It is interesting and instructive to consider why such gains are so common. As it turns out, the consistent application of principles of assessment FOR learning provides students with insights about their learning that, in turn, triggers productive emotional reactions. This consideration of how the psychology of learning can be applied to boost achievement must also prompt us to think about how classroom assessment that is poorly done can have the opposite effect and trigger destructive emotional reactions in learners.

Learning Facilitators

When we begin instruction by sharing with students a version of the learning target that is easy for them to understand, it focuses them on their learning destination. There is no need for them to try to guess what success looks like—we used to call that "psyching out the professor" in college as we tried to figure out what to emphasize in our studies. This clarity of destination eliminates ambiguity about the meaning of success. The emotional result is a sense of security, of confidence—there will be no surprises.

By providing students with samples of work spanning the full range of quality from poor work to very good work at the beginning of their learning, we provide them with mile markers for tracking their journey toward success. Once again, this information minimizes that sense of vulnerability and uncertainty that students feel when they wonder, "Am I doing this right? Am I making appropriate progress?" By helping the learner to see the gap between "where I am now in relation to where I want to be" narrowing over time, we lay the foundation for growing confidence and an increased desire to succeed.

When we provide students with continuous access to descriptive (versus judgmental) feedback as they learn, we accomplish three things. First, we help them understand the keys to their own success in clear and specific language. This builds confidence. Second, we give them specifically action-able information they can use to improve the quality of their work—again, a confidence builder. And third, we allow them to experience the constructive positivity that comes with small increments of immediate success. The val-idation inherent in achieving any one of these improvements might be the one win they need to turn everything around; these ongoing wins can be the reinforcement that promotes persistence.

When we help students learn how to engage over time in ongoing self-assessment during their learning, we help them form a link between their actions and their own academic well-being. In other words, we build their sense of self-efficacy in the classroom. *And if that's not the emotional foundation of "lifelong learner proficiency," I don't know what is!* The hope is that all students will begin to see themselves as riding ongoing winning streaks, feeding their optimism and belief that "success is within reach for me if I keep trying." The hope, too, is that they will learn to sense when "just keep trying" won't be enough to get there—when they need some outside help and how to deter-mine whether that help is really working. All these skills promote a sense of internal control over one's chances of success. Sometimes I'm tempted to call this "assessment for confidence," or for optimism!

In the broadest sense, when we give students the opportunity to engage in these assessment FOR learning practices over time, we also help them learn to evaluate their interest in various kinds of achievement domains and their ability to succeed in different performance domains. This provides them a basis for short- and long-term educational planning. This is empowerment.

Learning Inhibitors

As a quick counterpoint, consider the problems that can arise when the prin-ciples of assessment FOR learning are violated:

- When students are left to guess about the learning target or the keys to hitting it, the result is frustration, confusion, anxiety, and unfocused, counterproductive action on their part as they try for success.
- When students see no way to navigate the gap between where they are now and ultimate success, again, anxiety reigns. For those with a

history of struggle, failure can seem inevitable. How do they even ask for help? What can the teacher do? Why even try? This is how students on chronic losing streaks fall prey to learned pessimism; this is how learning stops.

MOTIVATORS IN THE PERFECT SYSTEM

We have long operated assessment systems on the assumption that assessment is something adults do to students. It is that, and we adults need to do our part well, using high-quality assessments to gather dependable evidence for the basis of sound instructional decisions and to certify student achievement. But the insight of the assessment FOR learning research is that assessment is not limited to that one-way arrangement. Students, too, constantly monitor their own achievement and make crucial "data-based" instructional decisions based on their interpretation of their own successes or failures. Some of the decisions they make can be destructive ones, such as whether they are "smart" or not and whether to keep trying or not.

If students decide that success is beyond reach for them, the game is over before we adults ever get a chance to contribute. The key classroom assessment question for us is "Can we keep them believing in themselves and keep them willing to take the risk of trying?" My answer is yes, we can—by consistently applying the principles of assessment FOR learning so that students always know where they are headed, where they are now, and how they can close the gap between.

The bottom line here is that the student's emotional response to assessment results—whether his or her score is high, mid-range, or low—is what determines what that student will do about those results. In the perfect assessment system, when students see assessment results, their schooling processes must help them get to the place where they are able to say to themselves, "I understand these results, I know what do to next, and I'm OK. I choose to keep trying." What they cannot be left behind to say is what too many of them say now: "I have no idea what these results mean, I don't know what to do next, and I'm too stupid learn this stuff anyway. I give up."

A SUMMARY OF KEY ASSESSMENT/ MOTIVATION LINKS

What students think about and do with assessment results is at least as important as what we adults think about and do with those results. We can help students take responsibility for their own success by

- Adding students to our assessment user/instructional decision maker team as full partners.
- Making sure both we and they are crystal clear about the intended learning targets from the very outset of instruction, including the place of all targets in ongoing learning progressions.
- Mastering the basic principles of sound assessment practice so we can ensure the quality of all assessments and the dependability of the evidence they provide.
- Communicating assessment results in terms that learners understand in the context of the learning progressions they are trying to ascend.
- Helping learners see, understand, and feel in control of the changes in their own capabilities as these evolve over time.

When it comes to defining how educators can help students develop into lifelong learners, this is the only approach that makes sense to me.

THE COSTS AND
BENEFITS OF PERFECTION

There is no limit to how good you can get in pursuit of perfection.
                                                    —SACHIN KUMAR PULI

I have advanced challenges to several basic tenets of the assessment legacy of American education, contending that

- Accountability testing has not improved schools because it fails to serve the information needs of the instructional decision makers whose decisions drive school quality.
- Defining achievement expectations as domains of learning targets or achievement standards yields assessments that are of little instructional value because scores are too imprecise.
- For decades, we have ignored matters of assessment quality at important levels of use throughout our educational systems.
- Our communication of assessment results has been ineffective in delivering critical information into the hands of key assessment users and decision makers.
- Our systems for linking assessment to student motivation have caused as many students to give up in hopelessness as they have encouraged.

The perfect assessment system envisioned in this book can overcome these chronic problems. It is a local school district assessment system set up to provide specific remedies. It is *balanced* in that it generates assessment results for the purpose of supporting learning and for the purpose of certifying learning in the classroom and at school and district levels. But clearly the classroom level of assessment is the foundation, where the instructional decisions that contribute the most to student success and school quality are made.

In my vision of excellence in assessment, the role of state and federal education officials and agencies is to support the development of high-quality local assessment systems. Once established, local systems can generate all the evidence that state and federal officials need to fulfill their public accountability responsibilities—that is, to maximize school quality and equity.

In the perfect system, the focus of assessments is student mastery of individual, high-priority academic achievement standards, *not* mastery of broad domains of achievement. This shift requires the development of clear and appropriate learning progressions that are well articulated by teachers and well understood by students.

This perfect system promises to deliver dependable evidence of student mastery of standards by relying on high-quality assessments in every context. This means that everyone involved in the gathering and use of assessment results must bring to those processes a foundation of assessment literacy— that is, a confident, competent mastery of the principles of sound assessment.

Because of the critical link between assessment results and instructional decision making, in the perfect system, all assessment results are communicated to their intended users in a timely and understandable (read: immediately useable) form. This means results are delivered not as "data" that must be "unpacked" but as easy-to-interpret, actionable *information.* Truly effective communication is required.

Finally, permeating the perfect system is a keen sense that each student can be taught how to partner with the teacher to monitor and control his or her own academic progress. Consistent application of principles of assessment FOR learning maintains high levels of student motivation, engagement, and learning success. The shared goal for all is to build every student's lifelong learner confidence and achievement.

Figure 4 provides a concise summary of the key transitions from our outdated assessment legacy to a new, instructionally helpful vision of excellence in assessment.

FIGURE 4

Replacing Tired Assessment Dogma with Vital Instructional Relevance

Key to Sound Assessment	Leave Behind	Replace With
Clear Purpose	*Neglect of key users and uses*	*Balanced service to all users*
Primary reason for assessing:	Accountability	Maximum learning success
Intended user/decision maker:	Adult decision makers only	Students too
Key decision to be informed:	"Have students learned enough?"	"Are students growing?"
Clear Learning Targets	*Illusion of academic rigor*	*Clear achievement standards*
Definition of expectations:	Content domains	Specific learning targets
Organization of expectations:	Content within grade level	Learning progressions
Made available to:	Educators only	Students and families too
Quality Assessments	*For standardized tests only*	*For all assessments/contexts*
Activating focus:	Sample content domains	Fit to purpose/target context
Evaluation criteria:	Reliability and validity	Impact on learner too
Dominant method(s):	Multiple-choice formats; one-time administration for all	All available methods as needed; evidence accumulated over time
Assessment literacy required:	For professional test experts	For all engaged in assessment
Effective Communication of Results	*As dictated by requirements of the assessment process*	*As dictated by the decision to be informed*
To whom?	Adult decision makers	Students too
In what form?	Scores compared to cutoff	Standards mastered or not
Communicate how?	Numerical score or grade	Descriptive feedback when formative; judgmental when summative
Use Assessment to Motivate	*Many students give up in hopelessness*	*All students strive for success*
Motivate which students?	Those higher in rank order	Everyone at all levels of achievement
Motivate how?	Anxiety and intimidation	Learning success
Primary motivator:	Win the competition; finish higher than others	Become a competent lifelong learner

IT'S TIME TO RE-EVALUATE OUR ASSESSMENT VALUES AND BELIEFS

If we are to accomplish these transitions effectively, we will need to reconsider the societal and educational values and beliefs that have long guided our use of assessment in schools. Here are my keys to changing our assessment culture:

- **We must accept the societal change in the mission of our schools.** This means committing ourselves to the pursuit of universal academic success that leaves all students in possession of essential, lifelong learner proficiencies. From that foundation, each student will be prepared to find his or her own pace and pathways to the workplace training or college studies that meet his or her needs.

- **We must move beyond the long-standing belief that standardized achievement tests can pave the path to better schools.** They have not and will not, because they cannot. It is time for us to embrace the value that the road to excellence is paved with high-quality assessments designed and used to meet the needs of all users, but especially those who collaborate day to day in the classroom: students and their teachers.

- **We must the shift the spotlight, resources, and locus of assessment control from federal and state departments of education to local school districts.** Even as I write this, the federal government is compelling states to design new state accountability assessment systems under the Every Student Succeeds Act. If local systems are built well and function effectively, then the evidence of student learning success can be aggregated from local levels upward. Everything about the perfect assessment system described herein is designed to permit this kind of accountability.

- **We must embrace the power of balanced assessment systems at the local school district level.** We will not achieve excellence in assessment unless and until we honor the information needs of classroom, interim/benchmark, and annual assessment users and give them what they need to support and certify student achievement. Only then will the needs of all essential assessment users be honored.

- **We must wipe out the belief that the only assessments that must meet standards of quality are those that happen once a year.** Certainly, the assessment evidence used for accountability purposes must be of outstanding quality in order to serve assessment users, but so must day-to-day classroom and interim assessments used by practitioners to guide student learning. We must recognize and honor the need for a universal foundation of assessment literacy throughout the fabric of American education.

- **We must acknowledge that the foundation of any assessment is the set of learning targets to be assessed.** Without agreement on what it means to be academically successful in each relevant learning context, we have no basis for creating assessments capable of helping students succeed *or* capable of certifying their success. As difficult as it may be to attain agreed-upon standards for learning progressions, that is what we must force ourselves to identify and create. If we define standards at state, local, and classroom levels, we can accommodate differences of opinion about the meaning of academic success.

- **We must embrace a new role for students.** Assessment is *not* merely something adults do to students. We know that students constantly evaluate themselves and their chances of success. We know how to help them keep the faith and strive on. We must enlist students as full partners in the assessment process.

- **We must update our systems of communication about student achievement, acknowledging that keys to success vary with the context.** Grades and test scores may serve summative accountability purposes, but they fail us in formative contexts, where instructional decision makers need detail about student strengths and weaknesses to inform decisions about what comes next in the student's learning. We must commit to gathering, storing, and reporting the details of learning success for each student using readily available information management technologies to aggregate evidence when needed for accountability purposes.

IT'S TIME FOR ASSERTIVE ACTION (FACING THE COSTS)

Achieving such a profound shift in culture and building the perfect assessment system won't be easy or cost-free, but it is absolutely within reach. Here are the essential actions we must take:

- **Put in place comprehensive programs of professional development to build a universal foundation of assessment literacy throughout the education profession.** This includes providing teachers and their supervisors the opportunity to learn to build and use quality assessments and to apply the principles of assessment FOR learning so they can succeed at motivating all students to strive for academic success.

- **Train policymakers, school leaders, and communities in the benefits of productive and truly balanced LOCAL assessment systems.** Both preservice and inservice professional development for school administrators and teachers called for in the previous action will prepare them to begin to educate local school board members, state department personnel, and state and federal legislators. The National Parent Teacher Association (2016) has already launched such training programs for communities.

- **Allocate more resources for key assessment work to be done at the local level.** Local school district leaders need time, energy, and expertise to establish conditions necessary to achieve a balanced assessment system and meet the information needs of all assessment users.

- **Abandon domain sampling as a test development strategy and replace it with the assessment of individual achievement standards.** It is possible to aggregate evidence of the extent of student mastery of standards up from local school district databases to meet accountability needs at other levels. Thus, this data need can be served at a fraction of the cost of current accountability testing.

- **Agree across education agencies about our highest-priority achievement standards.** This includes finding agreement across districts within states for accountability at that level and agreement within local faculties about their definition of academic success. The work must include the development of learning progressions of standards. For standards to be held statewide, states must do this work in collaboration with districts. Districts must be responsible for progression building for the local priorities they add.

- **Plan for and develop digital libraries of high-quality assessments.** This kind of repository will collect and make available standards-referenced assessments that have been vetted for quality and are capable of meeting the information needs of a diverse array of classroom-, district-, and state-level assessment users.

- **Develop new information management systems for assessment results.** These systems will permit us to collect, store, retrieve, and communicate assessment results as each student ascends his or her relevant learning progressions. To the extent that state education agencies can assist in this development, information management systems can be designed for consistency across districts, schools, and classrooms. As students change districts, their records will accompany them.

THE BENEFITS WILL BE LEGION

At the end of Chapter 1, I promised that the new assessment vision I am presenting would deliver an array of immensely valuable benefits. Let me conclude by recounting that list in greater detail. I believe I have built the case for each of these statements.

- **All assessments at any level will fit into the same integrated assessment/information management system.** The foundation of that system will be agreed-upon high-priority achievement standards. Any assessment, whether state, local, or classroom, of any standard can contribute evidence of student mastery of that standard. Evidence from any source can be merged into the record for that student regarding that particular standard for corroboration.

- **Valuable assessment results will be available for all instructional decision makers in all contexts.** All relevant data-based instructional decisions can be made on the basis of dependable evidence on the current status of student learning at classroom, periodic, and annual levels of assessment for both formative and summative purposes.

- **We will have a continuous emphasis on assessment to support learning for each individual student working in collaboration with his or her teacher.** Attention is devoted to building relations between the individual student and teacher in the service of helping all students advance through their learning progressions. But the collection and summary of evidence of summative decision making will be readily available as well.

- **We will have unprecedented clarity of achievement expectations, locally and statewide.** Each state will have an agreed-upon, select set of highest-priority standards, which can be augmented at the local district or even school level. Fully articulated learning progressions for each of these targets will be available to focus districts, schools, teachers, students, and families on the pathway to successful learning.

- **We will have evidence that is immediately available and nothing but diagnostic.** The local basis of our assessment system and the specificity of results means diagnostic information will be immediately available for use in instructional decision making. Contrast that with months of waiting for statewide test results.

- **We will have precisely comparable evidence readily available for a wide range of purposeful analyses.** Immediately transferrable and interpretable academic records will exist for each student. Everyone will know at any point in time how each student is progressing and what comes next in that student's learning. Finally, assessment truly will be used to help manage instruction.

- **We will have easy access to the full range of assessment methods needed to measure student mastery of the simplest to the most complex learning targets.** Today, because our high-stakes testing vision has us administering once-a-year tests to tens or hundreds of thousands of students, it's necessary to rely on the most economical assessment method—machine-scored, multiple-choice tests—and to limit the learning targets we assess to those that are compatible with this method. The perfect assessment system can rely on a much broader range of assessment methods—including selected response, written response, performance assessment, and direct personal communication with the student—because large-scale mass testing is not required. This will permit assessment of the broadest possible array of complex learning targets.

- **We will have new flexibility in assessment administration.** Local verification of student mastery of standards can be conducted at any time during the year—whenever instruction focused on that standard is completed.

- **We will have results that are easy to interpret and act on by all users in all contexts.** Say goodbye to the myriad challenges that typically accompany highly technical and complex but "data rich" and hard-to-interpret content domain test scores. We will speak only of specific achievement standards mastered or not, and we will have the evidence to back it up.

- **We will be able to achieve excellence in communication of results both in formative and summative assessment situations.** Effective communication of results is crucial in each context, but the keys to effectiveness vary between them. Practitioners schooled in those differences will be ready to deliver results in a form that works regardless of the context.

- **We will have immediate communication of results instead of having to wait weeks or months for test scores.** When any assessment of any particular standard is conducted, it can be scored immediately using accompanying scoring schemes, and the results will be ready for the intended audience to act on.

- **All students will be motivated by the belief that academic success is within reach for them if they keep striving for it.** Consistent application of principles of assessment FOR learning will make this possible.

In short, my hope is that the kind of perfection I have described will promote smoothly operating local assessment systems that serve students, teachers, school leaders, and policymakers, as well as parents and school communities in general. We will be able to trust local assessors to provide dependable evidence in an economical manner as long as they can defend the quality of their assessments. We will be able to pool state and local assessment resources for flexible assessment development, administration, reporting, and use. State and local districts will be able to combine their resources for assessment development, administration, and interpretation. Contributions of assessments to assessment libraries can accumulate from all directions. Once created, each assessment can be reused as needed. This is just another way that this vision makes economic sense.

The perfect assessment system relies on sound assessment practice throughout, driven by sound assessment policy that makes efficient use of assessment resources. And, most important, it provides a feasible way for low-performing schools to narrow achievement gaps and reduce dropout rates through the careful management of the emotional dynamics of their students' assessment experiences.

It's time to move our assessment practices from the 1950s to the century we're living in. *It's time to invest in our teachers and local school leaders instead of investing in more tests.* It's time to help all students understand how to unleash their own strengths and gain a sense of themselves as learners capable of choosing their own pathways to success. We can help our students keep their dreams alive so that those dreams can come true.

APPENDIX

Resources for the Development of Assessment Literacy

The list provided here has been adapted, with permission, from a list of resources compiled by the Michigan Assessment Consortium.

Books

Brookhart, S. M. (2008). *How to give effective feedback to your students.* **Alexandria, VA: ASCD.**
This book provides principles, practical guidelines, and examples for creating and delivering feedback on student work.

Brookhart, S. M. (2013). *How to create and use rubrics for formative assessment and grading.* **Alexandria, VA: ASCD.**
One of the tricky aspects of creating a rubric is being sure it assesses student thinking, not student ability to follow directions. This guide provides a set of principles for writing or selecting rubric criteria and performance level descriptions that, together, describe a continuum of performance on important learning outcomes. Examples are included.

Brookhart, S. M. (2015). *Performance assessment: Showing what students know and can do.* **West Palm Beach, FL: Learning Sciences.**
A performance assessment is one that requires students to create a product or demonstrate a process or both, and uses observation and judgment based on

clearly defined criteria to evaluate the qualities of the work. Therefore, performance assessment has two parts: (1) a task and (2) a rubric. This book is a one-stop reference for information about performance assessment, combining how to design tasks and how to create rubrics (which author Brookhart treated separately in the two books above). It includes many examples.

Chappuis, J. (2015). *Seven strategies of assessment FOR learning* (2nd ed.). Hoboken, NJ: Pearson Education.

Here, you'll find a detailed analysis of classroom assessment strategies that help teachers help students know where they are headed in their learning, where they are now, and how to close the gap between the two. It also covers when and how to involve students in ongoing self-assessment in the service of learning success.

Chappuis, J., & Stiggins, R. (2017). *An introduction to student-involved assessment FOR learning* (7th ed.). Columbus, OH: Pearson Education.

This is an introduction to the principles of sound assessment for preservice teacher candidates.

Chappuis, J., Stiggins, R., Chappuis, S., & Arter, J. (2012). *Classroom assessment for student learning: Doing it right—using it well* (2nd ed.). Upper Saddle River, NJ: Pearson Education.

This book is a comprehensive inservice assessment learning guide for local educators focused on summative and formative assessment practices that are useful in the classroom and at the school level.

Chappuis, S., Commodore, C., & Stiggins, R. (2017). *Balanced assessment systems: Leadership, quality, and the role of classroom assessment* (4th ed.). Thousand Oaks, CA: Corwin.

This guide is organized to help local school district leadership teams evaluating their district's organization readiness to sustain a balanced, instructionally helpful assessment system—one that meets the information needs of all instructional decision makers.

Erkens, C. (2016). *Collaborative common assessments.* Bloomington, IN: Solution Tree.

This book presents professional development guidelines for teacher teams and school leaders interested in developing formative common assessments that can be used to evaluate and improve instruction.

Heritage, M. (2010). *Formative assessment: Making it happen in the classroom.* Thousand Oaks, CA: Corwin.

Teachers who are just beginning to think about formative assessment—why to do it and what it looks like in practice—will find this book to be a good starting place.

Heritage, M. (2013). *Formative assessment practice: A process of inquiry and action.* Cambridge, MA: Harvard Education Press.

This book provides a complete background on productive applications of formative assessment and particular help in the development of learning progressions.

Moss, C. M., & Brookhart, S. M. (2009). *Advancing formative assessment in every classroom: A guide for instructional leaders.* Alexandria, VA: ASCD.

This resource aims to clear up misconceptions about formative assessment, explaining it as an active and intentional learning process that partners teachers and students, and breaks it down to six elements that school leaders can explore with teachers to foster better understanding and effective implementation. Several specific formative strategies are provided, along with examples and instructive scenarios.

O'Connor, K. (2009). *How to grade for learning.* Thousand Oaks, CA: Corwin.

This book addresses most of the common problems teachers face in grading and provides commonsense solutions with strong rationales. It's a good source of strategies for transforming achievement information into grades.

Popham, W. J. (2010). *Everything school leaders need to know about assessment*. Washington, DC: Sage.

This book outlines the key assessment concepts that school administrators must understand about the assessments used in their schools—both summative assessments and formative assessment practices.

Popham, W. J. (2017). *Classroom assessment: What teachers need to know* (8th ed.). Boston: Pearson Education.

This is an introductory textbook on classroom assessment for teacher education programs.

Stiggins, R. (2009). Essential formative assessment competencies for teachers and school leaders. In H. L. Andrade & G. J. Cizek (Eds.), *Handbook of formative assessment*. New York: Routledge.

Part of a book on formative assessment, this piece outlines the classroom assessment competencies teachers need and school leaders must understand, as well as how such skills can be learned and used.

Stiggins, R. (2014). *Revolutionizing assessment: Engage students, inspire learning*. Thousand Oaks, CA: Corwin.

This is a guide to sound assessment practices designed for parents and the greater school community.

Wiliam, D. (2011). *Embedded formative assessment*. Bloomington, IN: Solution Tree.

This book explores practical classroom applications for formative assessment and evidence of the kind of positive impact they can have on student learning.

Articles

American Federation of Teachers, National Council on Measurement in Education, & National Education Association. (1990). Standards for teacher competence in educational assessment of students. *Educational Measurement: Issues and Practice, 9*(4), 30–32.

Brookhart, S. M. (2011, Spring). Educational assessment knowledge and skills for teachers. *Educational Measurement: Issues and Practices, 30*(1), 3–12.

Council of Chief State School Officers. (2013). InTASC model core teaching standards: A resource for state dialogue. Washington, DC: Author.

McMillan, J. H. (2000). Fundamental assessment principles for teachers and school administrators. *Practical Assessment, Research & Evaluation, 7*(8).

Michigan Assessment Consortium (2015). Assessment literacy standards—A national imperative. Lansing, MI: Author.

Online Resources

Assessment for Learning
http://www.assessmentforlearning.edu.au/default.asp?id=912
This website, developed by the Curriculum Corporation on behalf of the education departments of the States, Territories, and Commonwealth of Australia, contains professional learning modules (with video), example assessment tasks with samples of student work, and a brief research background (mostly a list of references).

Assessment Literacy Resources from the Iowa Department of Education
https://www.educateiowa.gov/pk-12/student-assessment/assessment-learning-formative-assessment#Assessment_for_Learning_Professional_Development
The "Formative Assessment Tips" make up a nice, brief compendium available to the public. There are also professional development modules available; registration is necessary.

Assessment Literacy Resources from the North Carolina Department of Public Instruction
http://www.dpi.state.nc.us/accountability/educators/vision/formative

North Carolina's Formative Assessment Learning Community's Online Network (NC FALCON) is an online professional development series of modules focused on components of formative assessment, including questioning, discussions, learning activities, feedback, conferences, interviews, and student reflections. Formative assessment is defined as at the classroom level, minute-by-minute, and not for grading.

Assessment Literacy Resources from the Northwest Evaluation Association (NWEA)

https://www.nwea.org/blog/category/assessment-basics/

Part of the *Teach. Learn. Grow.* education blog, this is a source for perspectives on assessment from a diverse group of experts.

Assessment Literacy Resources from the Ohio Department of Education

http://education.ohio.gov/Topics/Teaching/Educator-Evaluation-System/How-to-Design-and-Select-Quality-Assessments

This collection of resources focused on building assessment literacy includes an overview and modules on Depth of Knowledge, performance assessment, and assessment blueprints.

Assessment Training Institute

http://ati.pearson.com/

The Assessment Training Institute offers an annual conference on assessment, a number of specialized assessment seminars, and a number of print and video resources on assessment.

Classroom Assessment Standards

http://www.jcsee.org/the-classroom-assessment-standards-new-standards

This is a compendium of standards for educators, essentially defining assessment literacy. Although this resource tells educators what they need to know and be able to do, it does not provide educational materials to further that effort.

Information on Formative Assessment from the National Center on Educational Outcomes (NCEO)
https://nceo.info/Assessments/formative
This website emphasizes Universal Design and selecting appropriate accommodations, both of which are important for assessment of students with special needs.

Michigan Assessment Consortium (MAC)
http://www.michiganassessmentconsortium.org/
The MAC website contains information on assessment literacy, including the MAC's assessment literacy standards and information on assessment learning resources now under development.

REFERENCES

American Educational Research Association, American Psychological Association, & National Council on Measurement in Education. (2014). *Standards for educational and psychological testing.* Washington, DC: Authors.

Amrein, A. L., & Berliner, D. C. (2002). High stakes testing, uncertainty and student learning. *Educational Policy Analysis Archives, 10*(18). Retrieved from http://epaa.asu.ojs/article/view/297/423

Anderson, L. W., & Bourke, S. F. (2000). *Assessing affective characteristics in school* (2nd ed.). Mahwah, NJ: Erlbaum.

Black, P. (1986). Assessment for learning. In D. L. Nuttall (Ed.), *Assessing educational achievement* (pp. 1–18). London: Falmer Press.

Black, P., & Wiliam, D. (1998a). Assessment and classroom learning. *Assessment in Education, 5*(1), 7–74.

Black, P., & Wiliam, D. (1998b). Inside the black box: Raising standards through classroom assessment. *Phi Delta Kappan, 80*(2), 139–148.

Chappuis, J. (2015). *Seven strategies of assessment FOR learning* (2nd ed.). Columbus, OH: Pearson.

Chappuis, S., Commodore, C., & Stiggins, R. (2010). *Assessment balance and quality: An action guide for school leaders.* Columbus, OH: Pearson.

Chappuis, S., Commodore, C., & Stiggins, R. (2017). *Balanced assessment systems: Leadership, quality, and the role of classroom assessment.* Thousand Oaks, CA: Corwin.

Cizek, G. J. (2005). High-stakes testing: Contexts, characteristics, critiques, and consequences. In R. P. Phelps (Ed.), *Defending standardized testing* (pp. 23–54). Mahwah, NJ: Erlbaum.

College Board. (2015). *The SAT suite of assessments: Using scores and reporting to inform instruction.* New York: Author. Retrieved from https://collegeread-iness.collegeboard.org/pdf/redesigned-sat-k12-using-scores-and-report-ing-inform-instruction.pdf

Darling-Hammond, L., Amrein-Beardsley, A., Haertel, E., & Rothstein, J. (2012). Teacher evaluation. *Phi Delta Kappan, 93*(6), 8–15.

Dorr-Bremme, D. W., & Herman, J. L. (1986). *Assessing student achievement: A profile of classroom practices.* Los Angeles: UCLA Center for the Study of Evaluation.

Guild, P. (1994, May). The culture/learning style connection. *Educational Leadership, 51*(8), 16–21.

Hattie, J., & Timperley, H. (2007). The power of feedback. *Review of Educational Research, 77*(1), 81–112.

Heritage, M. (2010). *Formative assessment: Making it happen in classrooms.* Thousand Oaks, CA: Corwin.

Heritage, M. (2013). *Formative assessment practice: A process of inquiry and action.* Cambridge, MA: Harvard Education Press.

National Parent Teacher Association. (2016). *PTA ESSA Parent Roadmap.* Washington, DC: Author. Retrieved from https://pta.org/advocacy/essa.cfm?ItemNumber=5035&navItemNumber=5051

Oregon Department of Education. (2016). House Bill 2680 Work Group Report. Salem, OR: Author.

Oregon Education Association, Oregon Department of Education, & Oregon Education Investment Board. (2015). *A new path for Oregon: System of assessment to empower meaningful student learning.* Salem, OR: Authors. Retrieved from: https://www.oregoned.org/images/uploads/pages/3_3_2015_A_New_Path_for_Oregon_Proposal_by_Oregon_Educators_complete.pdf

Popham, W. J., & Ryan, J. M. (2012, April). Determining a high-stakes test's instructional sensitivity. Paper presented at the annual meeting of the National Council on Measurement in Education, Vancouver, BC, Canada.

Stiggins, R. J. (2014a). *Defensible teacher evaluation*. Thousand Oaks, CA: Corwin.

Stiggins, R. J. (2014b). Improve assessment literacy outside of school too. *Phi Delta Kappan, 96*(2), 67–72.

Stiggins, R. J. (2014c). *Revolutionize assessment: Empower students, inspire learning*. Thousand Oaks, CA: Corwin.

Stiggins, R. J., & Chappuis, J. (2017). *An introduction to student-involved assessment FOR learning* (7th ed.). Columbus, OH: Pearson Education.

Stiggins, R. J., & Conklin, N. (1992). *In teachers' hands: Investigating the practice of classroom assessment*. Albany, NY: State University of New York Press.

Wiliam, D. (2010). Standardized testing and school accountability. *Educational Psychologist, 42*(2), 107–122.

INDEX

ABOUT THE AUTHOR

Rick Stiggins is the founder and retired president of the Assessment Training Institute (ATI), Portland, Oregon, a professional development company created and designed to provide teachers, school leaders, policymakers, and communities with the assessment literacy they need to face the assessment challenges that pervade American education today. ATI is now owned by Pearson Education.

Prior to launching ATI in 1992, Stiggins served on the College of Education faculties of Michigan State University, the University of Minnesota, and Lewis and Clark College, Portland. He was director of test development at ACT in Iowa City, directed performance assessment and classroom assessment research and development programs at the Northwest Regional Educational Laboratory in Portland, and has been a visiting scholar at Stanford University and the University of Southern Maine.

After conducting a decade of in-school research on the state and status of classroom assessment in U.S. schools, Stiggins authored a leading and award-winning introductory textbook for teachers on classroom assessment, *An Introduction to Classroom Assessment FOR Student Learning*, now in its 7th edition with Pearson Education. He has created numerous other print, video, and online preservice and inservice training programs used by teachers, school leaders, and policymakers to improve assessment practice, and has published books, chapters, articles, and conference papers on classroom assessment research, development, and training.

Stiggins and his ATI team have helped hundreds of thousands of teachers and school leaders across the country and around the world learn to gather accurate evidence of student achievement and use the assessment process and its results to support, not merely to grade, student learning. The most unique aspect of their work is their practical development of the concept of "assessment FOR learning," a classroom practice that involves students in the self-assessment process while they are learning so they can have the confidence that success is within reach if they continue to strive for it.

Stiggins is a native of Canandaigua, New York, and a graduate of the State University of New York at Plattsburgh, where he majored in psychology. He also holds a master's degree in industrial psychology from Springfield (Mass.) College and a PhD in educational measurement from Michigan State University.

Details of Stiggins's work are available through his website, rickstiggins. com. He can be reached at rickstiggins@gmail.com.

Related ASCD Resources: Assessment

At the time of publication, the following ASCD resources were available (ASCD stock numbers appear in parentheses). For up-to-date information about ASCD resources, go to www.ascd.org. You can search the complete archives of *Educational Leadership* at www.ascd.org/el.

ASCD Edge Group
Exchange ideas and connect with other educators interested in assessment, grading, and assessment FOR learning at the social networking site ASCD EDge® at http://ascdedge.ascd.org.

Print Products
Advancing Formative Assessment in Every Classroom: A Guide for Instructional Leaders by Connie M. Moss and Susan M. Brookhart (#109031)

Charting a Course to Standards-Based Grading: What to Stop, What to Start, and Why It Matters by Tim Westerberg (#117010)

Grading Smarter, Not Harder: Assessment Strategies That Motivate Kids and Help Them Learn by Myron Dueck (#114003)

How Teachers Can Turn Data into Action by Daniel R. Venables (#114007)

How to Make Decisions with Different Kinds of Student Assessment Data by Susan M. Brookhart (#116003)

Instruction That Measures Up: Successful Teaching in the Age of Accountability by W. James Popham (#108048)

Rubrics for Formative Assessment and Grading (Quick Reference Guide—25 pack) by Susan M. Brookhart (#QRG117045P)

Teaching Students to Self-Assess: How do I help students reflect and grow as learners? (ASCD Arias) by Starr Sackstein (#SF116025)

Using Data to Focus Instructional Improvement by Cheryl James-Ward, Douglas Fisher, Nancy Frey, and Diane Lapp (#113003)

Video
The Power of Formative Assessment to Advance Learning (3 DVD Set and User Guide) (#608066)

For more information: send e-mail to member@ascd.org; call 1-800-933-2723 or 703-578-9600, press 2; send a fax to 703-575-5400; or write to Information Services, ASCD, 1703 N. Beauregard St., Alexandria, VA 22311-1714 USA.